Kickstart Package

KICKSTART

PACKAGE

TORBEN SØNDERGAARD

KICKSTART PACKAGE

By Torben Søndergaard

Kickstart Package / Torben Søndergaard

Paperback ISBN: 978-1-943523-93-1

ePub (iPad, Nook) ISBN: 978-1-943523-94-8

Mobi (Kindle) ISBN: 978-1-943523-95-5

PUBLISHED BY THE LAST REFORMATION
IN CONJUNCTION WITH THE LAURUS COMPANY, INC.

PUBLISHED IN THE UNITED STATES OF AMERICA

This book may be purchased in paperback from www.TheLastReformation.com, www.Amazon.com, and other retailers around the world.
Electronic versions are also available from their respective stores.

ACKNOWLEDGMENTS

Many thanks to ALL those who worked, edited, researched, and supported me in making this all possible.

I am eternally grateful to Josué Studer, whose hard work for two years on the "Kickstart Package" videos with graphics, video editing, and so much more. You are such a blessing!

I'm also immensely grateful for Marcia Neuhold, for taking the teachings from the "Kickstart Package" videos and recording them in this book.

A special thanks to Ever Calamaco for your help with the graphics and design in both this book and the workbook.

And a very special thank you to Asia Brazil Scoggins for editing, developing the layout, gathering, and formulating information from the "Kickstart Package" videos into both this book and workbook.

Finally, I want to thank Nancy E. Williams for genuinely being an amazing publisher and editor.

You all are a big blessing to me and the kingdom of God.
May many lives be changed forever because of this.
Thank you!

KICKSTART PACKAGE APP

Scan the QR Code to download the app to view the Kickstart Package videos, and to see other materials and videos to help you in your disciple walk.

TABLE OF CONTENTS

INTRODUCTION

Welcome to the **Kickstart Package**. I am Torben Søndergaard, and I am very excited to share this book with you. I truly believe it is full of the Word of God and will be a tool that will empower you and change your life forever. This book is for those who want to know the truth of the Gospel of Christ and how to live as a disciple of Jesus in everyday life.

To share a little about my background, I am from Denmark, and I did not grow up in a Christian family. Like most people living in Denmark, I was baptized as a baby in the tradition of the Lutheran church. I heard the Gospel of Jesus Christ for the first time on April 5, 1995. I repented and experienced the Holy Spirit entering my being. It marked the beginning of a new and amazing life with God. Since that day, I have spent time working on starting churches in different cities, and I have been traveling all over the world teaching and showing people how to live the life we read about in the Bible. God gave me a passion for equipping people to follow Jesus. He allowed me to start **The Last Reformation**, a movement that is spreading all around the world. Over the last years, I have had the honor of ministering to people in over 30 nations. I am currently living in America, where we are seeing God do amazing things. Aside from all of this, I am the author of six books and the producer of three movies that have been seen by millions of people.

One of the most incredible and transforming things we have been doing over the last few years is our Kickstart Weekends. A Kickstart Weekend is a three-day meeting with a strong focus on how to live the life we read about in the Bible. At these meetings, people learn about what the gospel is and how to share it, how to obey Jesus when it comes to healing the sick and casting out demons, and how to be led by the Holy Spirit. In a Kickstart Weekend, we give both teaching and demonstration. We teach, then we show people how to share it, and then everyone has the chance to obey Jesus in what they have learned. When we, for example, teach how to heal the sick, we take some people up to the front to pray for them, and after we have shown people how to do it, we let everyone pray for each other. After this, we send everyone out on the streets in small groups to do the same. This simple, biblical form of discipleship is very effective. We are not only called to read Jesus' Word, but to listen, learn, and obey it.

During a Kickstart Weekend, we often see many people become born again. They come to our Weekends thinking that they already know the Gospel, but they really don't. They have heard about Jesus and that He died for them, but they are often still holding on to their sins. They have never really understood what faith in Jesus is, the importance of repentance, and that after they have repented, they need to be baptized in water and with the Holy Spirit.

When people at our Kickstart Weekends hear the whole gospel and how they need to repent, get baptized in water and with the Holy Spirit, it changes their lives. When we then show them how they can teach this to others, pray for the sick, and cast out demons, it really changes everything. They are on fire and ready to share this with people around them. We have seen from that how quickly it goes from person to person. When everyone experiences freedom in Christ and then learns to go out and give it to others, it can spread very fast.

We have seen thousands of people become fully born again and transformed through our Kickstart Weekends. Afterward, they go home to spread the truth of the Gospel to the people around them.

You may be asking yourself why it is called a "kickstart weekend." Well, picture a motorbike with a kickstart lever. The motorcycle needs to be kickstarted for the motor to start running and for the motorcyclist to be able to start driving. This inspired me to call these meetings "Kickstart Weekends."

Throughout the years, I have seen tens of thousands of people join the Kickstart Weekends, and I have seen God use these meetings to radically change their lives. These kickstart weekends have been the most effective tool that we have seen thus far in producing disciples of Jesus. We have heard thousands of testimonies from people who have attended a Kickstart Weekend. Many of them have told us about how they were healed, set free, baptized in water and with the Holy Spirit, and how they have become fruitful disciples of Christ. We have seen God do so many incredible things at these meetings.

With the high effectiveness of the kickstart weekends being so evident, many people have said that they would like to host a kickstart weekend in their home. Therefore, over the last two years, we have been working on an amazing, life-changing video series called, **"The Kickstart Package."** This video series will provide you with clear and simple teaching that will give you the tools you need to be an effective disciple of Jesus. It will also give you the confidence and the tools needed for you to host your own kickstart weekends in your home, church, or elsewhere.

In this book, you will find the teaching that is being shared in the video series, plus answers to some of the possible questions you might have or that might be asked after seeing the video series or that you may be asked when hosting your own kickstart. For example, when you watch the teaching about baptism, someone may ask if they should get baptized again, or what about baptizing in the name of Jesus or the name of the Father, Son, and Holy Spirit? These are the kinds of questions that I desire to answer for you in this book. I encourage you to read this book and let the words transform your life. Then, you can consider hosting a kickstart in your home, church, or elsewhere. You can invite your neighbors, friends, people from your church, and anyone else who is interested. The combination of the video series and this book will provide you with everything you need.

Each of the seven (7) videos is approximately 40 to 50 minutes long, and you can easily host a kickstart weekend in two days. You and your guests can start the kickstart on Saturday at 10:00 a.m. and watch Lesson One (Disciple of Jesus) from 10:15 a.m. to 11:00 a.m. and Lesson Two (The New Birth) from 11:15 a.m. to 12:00 noon. At noon, you can take a lunch break. After this, watch Lesson Three (The Holy Spirit) from 1:30 p.m. to 2:15 p.m. and Lesson Four (The Good News) from 2:30 p.m. to 3:15 p.m. After the teaching, take the time to pray for those who need healing and baptize those who need to be baptized in water and with the Holy Spirit. In this book, we will try to give you as much help as possible, so that you who have never done this before are ready to step out in obedience and do this for the first time. So Saturday would be a day when you see people get born again and see lives transformed by the teaching, prayer, and baptisms.

On Sunday, meet again at 10:00 a.m. and watch Lesson Five (Knowing God) from 10:15 a.m. to 11:00 a.m. and Lesson Six (The Call of Jesus) from 11:15 a.m. to 12:00 noon. Once more, you and your guests can take a lunch break at noon. Then it is time to go out and practice what you have learned. From 1:30 p.m. to 4:00 p.m., go out and kickstart people on the streets (take people out on the streets to teach them how to share about Jesus and pray for healing for a stranger). After this, return to your place and let the people share what they experienced on the streets. Lastly, watch Lesson Seven (The Good Ground) from 4:30 p.m. to 5:15 p.m.

Together with this book and the videos, we also have a website called *KickstartPacket.com* where we will provide you with even more tools, videos, and everything you need to go forward with this life. If you would like to host your own kickstart but don't feel ready for it, you can also find people on our website who are ready to come and help you host it.

We also share on our website amazing testimonies from people who have attended a kickstart or hosted their own kickstart.

We believe that God will use this book to transform your life and then help you to experience the amazing life we read about in the Bible. We also believe that it will give you what you need to help others experience the same.

We hope you are ready to start your life as a disciple of Jesus Christ. And we hope you are ready to help us make disciples by hosting your own kickstart or by spreading the video series and book to other people.

God bless you.

— Torben Søndergaard
A disciple of Jesus Christ

DISCIPLE OF JESUS

LESSON ONE

Welcome to **Lesson One**, the first of seven lessons in this **Kickstart Package**. In this lesson, we will be looking at what it means to be a disciple of Jesus and how a disciple's life should look. I would like to start off this lesson by looking at the Bible and some of its contents.

The Bible is made up of 66 books. There are 39 books in the Old Testament and 27 in the New Testament. The New Testament starts with the Gospels—Matthew, Mark, Luke, and John. Following the Gospels is the Book of the Acts of the Apostles. After the Book of Acts, there are 21 letters written by Paul, James, Peter, John, and Jude. The Book of Revelation is at the end of the New Testament. This book is about the end times.

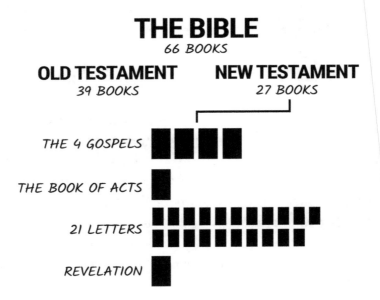

THE BIBLE
66 BOOKS

OLD TESTAMENT
39 BOOKS

NEW TESTAMENT
27 BOOKS

THE 4 GOSPELS

THE BOOK OF ACTS

21 LETTERS

REVELATION

I would now like to focus on the Book of Acts.

Throughout the centuries, Christianity has sadly moved far away from what it was originally intended to be. The traditions of man have, over the centuries, changed the simple and powerful life with Jesus into a life of traditions and church culture. For us to understand how it all started and how it should be today, God has given us the Bible and, especially, the Book of Acts. The Book of Acts is like a diary belonging to the early disciples, and it is a very special book because it is the only historical book in the Bible that shows us how they obeyed Jesus, how they shared the Gospel, and how people responded to it. Yes, the Book of Acts shows us how the early disciples preached the Gospel, cast out demons, healed the sick, and baptized people in water and with the Holy Spirit. We don't see these things in any other book in the Bible. Why? Well, the answer is simple. It is because the four Gospels (Matthew, Mark, Luke, and John), were written before Jesus died on the cross and before the Holy Spirit was sent down to earth on the day of Pentecost.

The four Gospels show how Jesus walked around, what He preached, what He did, and how He called His disciples to follow Him. In the Gospels, you also see how Jesus died on the cross and rose up again. Yes, you see many amazing things in the Gospels, but we do not see how the disciples lived after the cross and how they followed Jesus as born again believers, like you and me. The Gospels record the period before the cross, and therefore, we don't see anyone receive the Holy Spirit or get baptized in the name of Jesus. Because of this, the Gospels do not provide a clear picture of how we, as followers of Jesus, are supposed to live.

The letters following the Book of Acts, are written to people who have already become Christians/disciples. In these letters, we read about the church life and the problems it faced, but we don't read how people came to faith, what they did when they came to faith, and how they obeyed Jesus in their everyday lives. Because the letters were all written to people who were already Christians/disciples, they were written to people who have already repented, been baptized, and received the Holy Spirit. Because of this, we do not see how people came to faith or how the early disciples preached the Gospel in the letters. The only place we see that is in the Book of Acts.

The Bible teaches that Jesus has not and never will change. Hebrews 13:8 (NKJV) states, *"Jesus Christ is the same yesterday, today, and forever."* This verse also means that the Holy Spirit (the Spirit of Jesus) has not and will never change. The Holy Spirit is the same yesterday, today, and forever. Because of this, we can conclude that what we read in the Book of Acts is not only for the disciples of the early church, but it is also for us today. This means that, today, we can also experience what the early disciples experienced in the Book of Acts.

One of my favorite verses in the Bible is located in Acts 9. Acts 9:10-19 (NIV) states:

Now there was a certain disciple at Damascus named Ananias; and to him the Lord said in a vision, "Ananias." And he said, "Here I am, Lord." So the Lord said to him, "Arise and go to the street called Straight, and inquire at the house of Judas for one called Saul of Tarsus, for behold, he is praying. And in a vision he has seen a man named Ananias coming in and putting his hand on him, so that he might receive his sight." Then Ananias answered, "Lord, I have heard from many about this man, how much harm he has done to Your saints in Jerusalem. And here he has authority from the chief priests to bind all who call on Your name." But the Lord said to him, "Go, for he is a chosen vessel of Mine to bear My name before Gentiles, kings, and the children of Israel. For I will show him how many things he must suffer for My name's sake." And Ananias went his way and entered the house; and laying his hands on him he said, "Brother Saul, the Lord Jesus, who appeared to you on the road as you came, has sent me that you may receive your sight and be filled with the Holy Spirit." Immediately there fell from his eyes something like scales, and he received his sight at once; and he arose and was baptized. So when he had received food, he was strengthened. Then Saul spent some days with the disciples at Damascus.

As we read in this chapter, Paul (who, at the time, was called Saul) was against Jesus and His followers. Paul went to Damascus and gave a letter to the synagogue there to ask for permission to capture those who believed in Jesus and to bring them back to Jerusalem to imprison them. On his way to Damascus, a great light came from heaven, and when Paul saw it, he fell to the ground. He then heard a voice from heaven say, "Saul, Saul, why do you persecute me?" Paul then asked, "Who are you, Lord?" And the voice from heaven answered, "I am Jesus whom you are persecuting." After this, Paul was blinded. Paul was brought to a house where he fasted and sought God for three days. We then arrive at one of my favorite verses in the Bible: Acts 9:10 (NKJV), which states, *Now there was a certain disciple at Damascus named Ananias; and to him the Lord said in* a vision, "Ananias." And he said, "Here I am, Lord." If you continue reading, you will read that God spoke to His disciple, Ananias, and told him that he should go and pray for Paul. When Ananias arrived at the house where Paul was staying, he laid his hands on Paul, and Paul's eyes were healed, and he could see again. He then preached the Gospel to Paul, and Paul got baptized in water and received the Holy Spirit.

You may be wondering why one of my favorite verses in the Bible is Acts 9:10. I love this verse because the word "disciple" is used. The Bible does not say that there was a big prophet or priest in Damascus who had a special calling. No, the Bible says that there was a disciple in Damascus named Ananias, a disciple like you and me. And to that disciple, God spoke. I love this verse because it shows how God wants to speak to you and me today. That day, when Ananias prayed for Paul, he experienced four things. Ananias experienced (1) how God spoke to him, (2) how he was led by the Holy Spirit, (3) how he laid hands on Paul and saw him get healed in the name of Jesus, and lastly, (4) how he baptized Paul in water and with the Holy Spirit. Today, you and I can experience the same things Ananias did because that is the normal Christian life. We don't know a lot about who Ananias was, but the Bible makes it clear that he was a disciple like you and me.

Do you believe what Ananias experienced that day with Paul was the first time he had experienced these things? Do you believe that it was the first time he heard from God? Do you believe that it was the first time he was led by the Holy Spirit? Do you believe that it was the first time he laid hands on someone who got healed, or the first time he baptized someone in water and with the Holy Spirit? No, of course not. This was just one day in Ananias' life. Just because we don't read more about Ananias' life, it doesn't mean that Ananias did not experience these things in his daily life. I believe that Ananias heard from God, was led by the Holy Spirit, healed the sick, preached the Gospel, baptized people in water and with the Holy Spirit on a regular basis. I actually believe that we could write a whole book on Ananias' life and what he experienced with God, and I believe that we could also do the same with the twelve disciples and the seventy that Jesus called later. I believe that we could write a whole book on the lives of each of the 3,000 people who got baptized on the day of Pentecost. And I also believe that, as followers of Jesus, we should also be able to write a book about our life and that it should look very similar to what we read in the Book of Acts.

I know that life looks much different today compared to the time when Jesus walked on earth. We have cars, Internet, and a lot of things that people did not have back then. But, despite these differences, the Holy Spirit is still the same. What we read in the Book of Acts should be the normal Christian life. Jesus, in Mark 16:17-18 (NKJV) says, *"And these signs will follow those who believe: In My name they will cast out demons; they will speak with new tongues; they will take up serpents; and if they drink anything deadly, it will by no means hurt them; they will lay hands on the sick, and they will recover."* The problem that keeps many people from living the normal Christian life as depicted in the Book of Acts is religion. In the Bible, we do not read about babies being baptized, and we don't read about those babies later growing up and getting confirmed like we see in the Lutheran church today.

Take the time to reflect on your life. If you wrote a diary of your life, would it look like the Book of Acts? If not, then there is something wrong. We need to build our understanding of what the Christian life should look like upon the Word of God and not upon religion, culture, past experience, education, doctrines and traditions of men, and so on. Many years ago, I remember reading through the Book of Acts and then comparing it to what my life looked like. When I did this, I realized that my life looked very different from what I read in the Book of Acts. I realized that although I call myself a "Christian," my life looked nothing like the lives of the early disciples. In that moment, I understood that there was something wrong with the way I was living and that I had been deceived by religion. And when I understood this, things started to change. Now, when I compare my life to what I read in the Book of Acts, my life and the life of the early disciples look the same.

The Bible is the Truth, and that is what we need to build our foundation on. We need to understand that we do not need to be a prophet or apostle to experience the things we read about in the Book of Acts. It is not about being someone special. No, it is about being a disciple of Jesus, like Ananias. It is about living for and obeying Jesus, spreading the Gospel, being led by the Holy Spirit, healing the sick, and casting out demons. And God has called you to do this. He has called you to be His disciple. If you decide that you want to live the normal Christian life, you can experience the same things that I, Ananias, and many other people around the world have experienced. Yes, you can experience God speaking to you and guiding you by His Holy Spirit. You can experience praying for the sick and seeing them healed. And you can experience baptizing people in water and with the Holy Spirit. You can see some of these things in **The Last Reformation** movies or YouTube videos

Let us now look at two words in the Bible. The first is the word "Christian," and the second is "disciple." Did you know that the word "Christian" is written only three times in the entire Bible? Jesus never used the word "Christian." We first see "Christian" appear in the Bible eleven years after Jesus walked on earth, in Acts 11:26 (NKJV) , which states, "… And the disciples were first called Christians in Antioch." "Disciple," however, is written over 250 times in the Bible. Wow! Maybe we should stop using the word "Christian." Today, the word "Christian" is greatly misunderstood. You have probably heard people tell you, "I am a Christian, but I don't really live as one," or "I am a Christian in my own way." You have probably also heard people tell you, "I am a Christian because I go to church and try to live a good life." But try replacing the word "Christian" with the word "disciple." Now imagine if someone said to you, "I am a disciple of Jesus, but I don't really live as one," or "I am a disciple of Jesus in my own way." Again, imagine they said, "I am a disciple of Jesus because I go to church, and I try to live a good life." It sounds wrong, doesn't it? It would not make sense because we know that you must follow Jesus in order to be His disciple. You cannot become a disciple of Jesus just by going to church and trying to live a good life, and you cannot become His disciple in your own way. So maybe, like Jesus, we should not use the word "Christian."

X3 ■■■
CHRISTIAN

X250

What does the word "disciple" mean? Today, it is a word that we only use in churches, and it can cause people who are not Christian to become confused if you were to tell them that you are a disciple of Jesus. However, in Jesus' time, "disciple" was a very common word, and people understood what it meant. During Jesus' time on earth, there were many people who, like Jesus, had disciples. For example, the Pharisees, John the Baptist, and Moses all had disciples. So if we want to use another word other than "Christian" to describe followers of Jesus, "disciple" or "apprentice" would be good alternatives.

Being a disciple is being an apprentice. For example, some years ago, I worked as an apprentice in a bakery for three and a half years. At the time, I did not know how to bake anything. But I had my teacher/master (the baker) who was there to train and teach me to one day be able to bake like him. In the beginning, it was very challenging. I had moments when I thought I would never be able to bake like him, but, eventually, I learned, and I became better and better. Yes, eventually, I started to look more like my master (the baker), and in the end, I was almost as good of a baker as he was. Yes, I made many mistakes throughout my apprenticeship, but that is normal, and it is part of learning. It is okay to make mistakes, but it is not okay if you do not try. And it is the same with Jesus. We are Jesus' apprentices/disciples, and when we start an apprenticeship/discipleship with Him, we agree to follow Him, learn from Him, and become more and more like Jesus, our master, every day. Jesus, in Luke 6:40 (NKJV), states, *"A disciple is not above his teacher, but everyone who is perfectly trained will be like his teacher."*

Imagine I worked as an apprentice in a bakery for three and a half years, and at the end of my apprenticeship, I still did not know how to bake anything. Yes, imagine if I had not tried to bake anything myself, but that the whole time I was there, I only stood by and watched my master bake things. If this had been the case, there would have been something wrong with that bakery, my apprenticeship, my master, or me. Why? It is because the whole point of accepting an apprenticeship is so that, after a few years, I could be a real baker, like him. There is also something wrong if you have been a Christian/disciple/apprentice for ten years and still don't know how to do what Jesus has called you to do. We are called to be like Jesus. We are called to speak like Him, to be led by the Holy Spirit like Him, to heal the sick and cast out demons like Him, to serve like Him, to love like Him, and so on.

If you have been a Christian/disciple/apprentice for ten years and still have not learned how to do what Jesus has called you to do, there is something wrong. But don't worry because I believe that God can use this book to help you. I believe that God can use this book to help you start to live as a disciple/apprentice of Jesus. I want to help you to write a diary of your own life that looks like the Book of Acts. I really desire for you to live the life that Jesus wants you to live. But you need to be willing to obey Jesus. I cannot obey Him for you; that is your task. I can help teach and train you, but you need to step out in obedience and obey Jesus.

As I have previously said, I made many mistakes working as an apprentice in a bakery. And it was the same for the disciples of Jesus. There were times when Jesus' disciples were not able to do what Jesus wanted them to do. One example of this is in Matthew 17. In Matthew 17, we read about a man who brought his son, an epileptic, to Jesus' disciples because he wanted them to heal his son. Matthew 17:16-17 (NKJV) states, *"So I brought him to Your disciples, but they could not cure him."* Then Jesus answered and said, *"O faithless and perverse generation, how long shall I be with you? How long shall I bear with you? Bring him here to Me."* Later, we read how they brought the boy to Jesus and how Jesus healed him and set him free. Interestingly, Jesus did not say, *"... O faithless and perverse generation..."* to the boy or his father. No, He said that to His disciples because He was frustrated at them for not doing what they were supposed to do.

When I think about this story in Matthew 17, I think back to my time as an apprentice and how angry my master (the baker) would become when I forgot to put an ingredient in the bread or when I left something in the oven too long. Yes, I remember him rebuking me and shouting, "Torben, how long shall I put up with you? You should have learned by now." But I learned and became better, and that is the whole point of an apprenticeship. So our goal is to be, like Jesus, perfect, but we are on a journey, and you will make mistakes. And it is okay if we do not look exactly like Jesus now. But it is not okay if we don't look more like Him now than we did last year. Why? Well, because we are Jesus' apprentices, and we are supposed to be learning from Him and growing to be more like Him.

When a person accepts Jesus, they agree to an apprenticeship/discipleship where they must learn to be like Jesus. Accepting Jesus does not mean that you are supposed to go to church year after year and never learn how to do the things Jesus has called you to do. No, that is religion. And Jesus did not come to bring religion. Jesus came to help you follow Him as His disciple through the power of the Holy Spirit. Being born again (repenting, and being baptized in water and with the Holy Spirit) is the first step to being an apprentice/disciple of Jesus because we cannot walk like Jesus, or be like Jesus, if we do not have the power of the Holy Spirit.

Some years ago, while I was living in Denmark, I was on a Danish debate television program with a famous Danish Muslim and a famous Danish Jew. After the debate program finished, I sat down with the famous Danish Muslim and asked her some questions. I said to her, "Tell me about your faith and about what God is doing in your life." She was surprised by my question and answered, "It feels good when I read the Quran and when I pray in the mosques." "Tell me more. How does God speak to you?" I asked her. She answered, "It feels good when I read the Quran and when I pray in the mosques." I then told her, "Tell me more. How does God give you dreams? How does God lead you?" Again, she said, "It feels good when I read the

Quran and when I pray in the mosques." I continued and said, "Tell me more. How are people healed through you and how do you set people free?" Once again, she answered the same thing. That was the only answer she could give me for every question I asked her. Then, she asked me, "What about your life with God?" I then started to explain how I met God, how the Holy Spirit came into my life, how God speaks to me, how the Holy Spirit leads me, how I pray for the sick and they are healed, how I cast out demons, and how I get visions and dreams from God. I also told her about my relationship with God and what I have experienced with Him. She continued to ask me questions, and we ended up talking for one and a half hours. On that day, it became very clear to me that there is a huge difference between religion and relationship. She had a religion, but I had a relationship with God. And sadly, for many Christians, their Christianity is just a religion.

If I were to say to Christians who believe in Jesus and go to church, "Tell me about your life. How does God use you," they would likely give an answer similar to the famous Danish Muslim and say, "It feels good when I pray and when I go to church." If I would say to them, "Tell me about how the Holy Spirit leads you. How does God heal through you?" Again, many would say, "It feels good when I pray and when I go to church." Their answer would be similar to the famous Danish Muslim because they have a religion and not a relationship with God. It is important to understand that Jesus came to bring a relationship and not religion.

In Matthew 23:25-26 (NKJV), Jesus spoke to some of the religious leaders, *"Woe to you, scribes and Pharisees, hypocrites! For you cleanse the outside of the cup and dish, but inside they are full of extortion and self-indulgence. Blind Pharisee, first cleanse the inside of the cup and dish, that the outside of them may be clean also."* From this verse, you can clearly see a big difference between religion and relationship. True Christianity is from the inside out; it cleanses and changes you so that it will be visible to everyone around you that you follow Jesus. True Christianity is about being born again, becoming Jesus' apprentice/disciple and having a relationship with the living God. It is about becoming a new creation and being set free from the bondage of sin to start a new, holy, supernatural life with God while being led by His Spirit. True Christianity is about understanding that we, as followers of Jesus, are the Church and that we are temples of the Holy Spirit who lives inside of us.

Today, my life looks so much like the Book of Acts. And your life can look like that, too. It will be a journey, but it will be an amazing journey. I hope you are ready to follow Jesus as His disciple/apprentice. But first, you need to be born again. You need to be born again, and you need the Holy Spirit because, without Him, you cannot live this life. This is what we are called to do. The normal Christian life is to be a disciple of Jesus and to live the life we read about in the Book of Acts. Yes, in the beginning, we will make many mistakes, but we will learn and grow from those mistakes. So I hope you are ready to follow Jesus and to learn to live the life He desires for you. I hope you are ready to experience many amazing things with Him in your daily life.

QUESTIONS & ANSWERS

ARE YOU DECEIVED?

For you who are reading this book, I know that many of the things said in this book can be very challenging for you, depending on what church tradition you have grown up in. I would, therefore, like to address a little bit about deception. We need to understand that it is not enough for us to be sincere in our faith. We can be sincere and still be deceived. I have met many Mormons who are very sincere in their faith, but they are still deceived. They were told another gospel, a gospel that cannot save them. I have also met many Jehovah's Witnesses, and they are also very sincere in their faith and very active in spreading their faith, but they are still deceived. Why? It is because they have believed a different gospel.

When I look at my life now, I can see that I was also, at one time, deceived like those I mentioned. I was also taught another gospel that could not save me. I thought that I was a Christian because I was baptized as a baby and confirmed in the church. But that was a lie. The Bible does not say that you are born again because you were baptized as a baby and are a member of a church. I could have been the most sincere follower in the Lutheran church I attended, but I still would have been deceived. It is not enough to be sincere; you also need to have the right gospel and to do what the Bible says you need to do to be born again in order to follow Jesus. And I want to tell you the same thing. It is not about the sincerity of your faith. You can be the most sincere churchgoer and still be deceived. We, as Christians, need to be more like the Bereans who examined the Scriptures every day to see if what was said is the truth (Acts 17:11). We need to check the Scriptures ourselves and stop blindly following what we have been told.

I want to challenge you to ask questions about what you have been told up until now. Yes, I want you to question your traditions and what you have been told in your church. Does it match with what the Word of God says? You should also ask questions about what I am teaching you in this book. Yes, take your Bible and see if what I am saying is correct. We should do this with everyone so that we don't end up standing in front of God and finding out that we have been deceived.

CHRISTIAN OR DISCIPLE?

I hope this first lesson will challenge you and encourage you to ask yourself some very important questions. Ask yourself, "Am I a Christian, or am I a disciple? Does my life look like the life of Ananias or the other disciples I read about in the Book of Acts?"

After I had been a Christian for six years, I one day took the Bible and looked in the Book of Acts and compared it to my life. When I did that, I was completely shocked. I saw that I was deceived in many ways and that my life looked nothing like what I read in the Book of Acts. Yes, my life looked good when I compared it to the other people in the church, but we should not use our churches or traditions as the standards by which to evaluate our lives. At the same time, God opened my eyes to see how wrong I was and how deceived many others were in our church. Yes, we were building more on our church traditions than on what the Word was saying. During this time, I came across a parable of Jesus located in Luke 13:6-9 (NKJV) that states:

He also spoke this parable: "A certain man had a fig tree planted in his vineyard, and he came seeking fruit on it and found none. Then he said to the keeper of his vineyard, 'Look, for three years I have come seeking fruit on this fig tree and find none. Cut it down; why does it use up the ground?' But he answered and said to him, 'Sir, let it alone this year also, until I dig around it and fertilize it. And if it bears fruit, well. But if not, after that you can cut it down.'"

This parable speaks about a tree that did not produce fruit for three years and how the gardener wanted to cut it down. But the man told the gardener to give it one more year and that if it didn't produce fruit by then, he should cut it down. When I read this, it was like I heard God say, "Torben, you are this fig tree." But I had not been a "Christian" for three years without producing fruit; I was a "Christian" for six years without producing fruit. I realized that I was not a true disciple of Jesus and that I had no fruit in my life. And in the same way that Jesus, in the parable, gave the fig tree one more year to produce fruit, I told God that if I didn't bear any fruit by next year, that He should take my life. I know that it seems very radical, but my heart was really convicted, and I, at that moment, understood how important it is to bear fruit.

Jesus says in John 15:2 (NKJV), "Every branch in Me that does not bear fruit He takes away; and every branch that bears fruit He prunes, that it may bear more fruit." I told God, "God, I will give everything to you and obey you, and if I don't bear fruit one year from now, then you can take my life. On the same day I said this, I started a 40 day fast, and I saw my life begin to be transformed. And one year later, my life was completely changed. Yes, one year later, I was not a "Christian" without fruit, but a fruitful disciple who was following Jesus.

My hope for you who are reading this book is that you will not just read it, move on, and forget about it. No, I really want this to be a book that stirs something up inside of you and that encourages you to step out and obey Jesus. I want to see you get transformed into a fruitful disciple of Christ who will follow Him in your daily life. What will you do with the call that Jesus has given you? What will you do with the words you are reading in this book? It is totally up to you.

WHAT IF I CANNOT LIVE UP TO THIS LIFE?

When we read the Bible, we can see that being a disciple of Christ is about denying ourselves and taking up our cross. We see that a disciple is someone who obeys God in preaching the Gospel to others, healing the sick, casting out demons, living a holy and righteous life, and more. And being a disciple also includes obeying what Jesus says in Matthew 11:28-30 (NKJV), which states, *"Come to Me, all you who labor and are heavy laden, and I will give you rest. Take My yoke upon you and learn from Me, for I am gentle and lowly in heart, and you will find rest for your souls. For My yoke is easy and My burden is light."* We also need to obey Jesus by going to Him to receive rest. The call that Jesus has given us should not feel like a heavy burden because when we give everything to Him, He will transform us from the inside out, and all of the things He has called us to do, He will do in us. Yes, He will transform you, and you will not have to do things on your own strength. He will never call you to do something that He will not give you the strength to do. So don't worry and think that you cannot live up to being a disciple of Jesus. Follow Jesus and let Him transform your life. The rest will come naturally.

IS IT NOT ALL ABOUT WORKS?

The Bible makes it clear that faith without works/obedience is dead. James 2:26 (NKJV) states, *"For as the body without the spirit is dead, so faith without works is dead also."* But the Bible also makes it clear that the works it is talking about here in James are not works by the law. We don't become righteous by obeying the law. The gift that God has given us is free for everyone. And you can read this in Ephesians 2:8-9 (NKJV), which states, *"For by grace you have been saved through faith, and that not of yourselves; it is the gift of God, not of works, lest anyone should boast."* This verse makes it clear that, as believers, we are not saved by works of the law, but that it is by the grace of God that we are saved through faith and not through works so that we have nothing we can boast about. The next verse, Ephesians 2:10 (NKJV), states, *"For we are His workmanship, created in Christ Jesus for good works, which God prepared beforehand that we should walk in them."* But again, it is not talking about works by the law, nor is it saying that we should obey the law of Moses. No, these are works, as James is saying, that come out of obedience and a love for God.

So we come before God as we are, with nothing to offer Him, and it is by the grace of God that we are saved through faith in Jesus Christ. And when He comes and offers us salvation and transforms our lives, we, of course, desire to obey our Lord Jesus Christ. Why? It is because He has saved us, and we love Him and, therefore, want to obey Him. This is not obedience caused by a heavy burden, nor is it the works of trying to obey the law of Moses. It is works/obedience that comes through faith.

Today, there is an idea that we, as Christians, should not do any works, but that is so wrong. We need to obey. If you don't obey, then Jesus will say, *"But why do you call Me 'Lord, Lord,' and not do the things which I say?"* (Luke 6:46 NKJV). What about you? Do you obey Jesus? Just be honest with yourself and with Him. If we don't obey Him and do any works, why do we call Him Lord? The Bible makes it clear that those who are building the house on the rock are those who do not only listen to God's Word but that they also obey it. After Luke 6:46, Jesus continues in Luke 6:47-49 (NKJV) with saying:

"Whoever comes to Me, and hears My sayings and does them, I will show you whom he is like: He is like a man building a house, who dug deep and laid the foundation on the rock. And when the flood arose, the stream beat vehemently against that

house, and could not shake it, for it was founded on the rock. But he who heard and did nothing is like a man who built a house on the earth without a foundation, against which the stream beat vehemently; and immediately it fell. And the ruin of that house was great."

So to you who think that obedience is works and something we should not do, you are standing in a very dangerous place. Yes, we are free to obey the Law of Moses and free to obey Christ and His words. My advice to you is that you should take it one step at a time. Start to let Him transform your heart and get to know Him more. Then, the rest will come so much more naturally. And when it does, then you will not want to stop obeying Him, and it will not feel like a burden or hard work.

WHAT IF MY FAMILY AND THOSE AROUND ME BELIEVE IN SOMETHING DIFFERENT?

As you are going to see in this book, we will look at many things, including what it means to follow Jesus. Most of what I will say in this book will probably go against some of your traditions you have grown up in. But this is important because we have to come away from our traditions to obey Jesus and His Word.

I remember when I first heard the Gospel of Jesus Christ. My family and everyone else in my life were against it. My father forbade me to have anything to do with Jesus because it was so new to him, and he was afraid that his son had gone crazy. But I had a choice to make. I had to choose if I was going to obey my father or if I was going to obey what I knew deep down inside of me was the truth. I still remember looking at my father and thinking to myself, "Father, I love you, so therefore I will not do what you are saying because if I don't find the truth, who will share it with you? Yes, if I don't get Jesus, who can give Him to you?" And I made the decision to follow Jesus and obey Him instead of listening to what my family and everyone else around me said. My father was not happy about my choice, and over the next four or five years, he was very sad, disappointed, and sometimes even angry that his son had become what he called "brainwashed." But eventually, my father started to see a deep transformation in my life. And from seeing what God did in my life, he knew that Jesus was the Truth. One day, he repented. I baptized him in water, and when I laid my hands on him, he was filled with the Holy Spirit. From that day on, my father was a changed man. After this, he was so thankful that I did not listen to him when he forbade me to have anything to do with Jesus. Yes, he was so thankful that I chose to follow the truth and not listen to him at that time. And I want to encourage you to do the same, even if your family and friends think you are crazy. Always choose to follow the truth, no matter what others around you say, because it is the truth. And if it is the truth for you, it is also the truth for them. Maybe they don't see that right now, but if you truly love them, then help them to get the truth. Help them to get Jesus. And how can you do that if you don't have Him?

The Word of God will never change. People's opinions and ideas can change, and so can their traditions, but the Word of God will forever be the same. Some people will probably not understand your choice, and there will likely be people around you who will try and argue with you about your faith. But we cannot please everyone, so let's choose to please God, and let's decide to build our foundation on the truth, on Jesus. Let the truth not only set you free, but also all those around you.

When people don't like you because you choose to follow Jesus that is okay. Jesus actually spoke about this many times throughout the Bible, so don't be surprised when it happens. For example, in Matthew 10:34-39 (NKJV), Jesus talks about how He came to bring a sword to this world and not peace by saying:

Do not think that I came to bring peace on earth. I did not come to bring peace but a sword. For I have come to "set a man against his father, a daughter against her mother, and a daughter-in-law against her mother-in-law"; and "a man's enemies will be those of his own household." He who loves father or mother more than Me is not worthy of Me. And he who loves son or daughter more than Me is not worthy of Me. And he who does not take his cross and follow after Me is not worthy of Me. He who finds his life will lose it, and he who loses his life for My sake will find it.

Jesus also talks about how the world will hate His followers by stating in John 15:18-20 (NIV):

If the world hates you, keep in mind that it hated me first. If you belonged to the world, it would love you as its own. As it is, you do not belong to the world, but I have chosen you out of the world. That is why the world hates you. Remember what I told you: "A servant is not greater than his master." If they persecuted me, they will persecute you also. If they obeyed my teaching, they will obey yours also.

Throughout your life of following Jesus, you will experience that some people will leave you and no longer want to be your friend, but you will meet new people who will want to connect with you and who also, like you, serve Jesus. It has cost me a lot to follow Jesus, and although I have lost a lot, I have gained so much more than I could have ever imagined. So don't be afraid. Follow Jesus, and you will see that He will take care of the rest, as He says in Mark 10:28-30 (NIV):

Then Peter spoke up, "We have left everything to follow you!" "Truly I tell you," Jesus replied, "no one who has left home or brothers or sisters or mother or father or children or fields for me and the gospel will fail to receive a hundred times as much in this present age: homes, brothers, sisters, mothers, children and fields—along with persecutions—and in the age to come eternal life."

A REVELATION ABOUT BEING A DISCIPLE

For me, understanding that I am a disciple of Jesus and that being a disciple is like being an apprentice has changed everything. It has helped me to not be afraid of making mistakes. Why? Well, because it is normal for an apprentice to make mistakes. I am also not afraid to try because a disciple is someone who needs to try. I realize that I look more like Christ now than I did last year.

I want to tell you that it is so important that you not compare yourself with other people. Some people have been disciples for only a few months, others for a few years. And some people have been disciples for many years. We should not compare ourselves with others because we are all at different places in our journey with God. But it is important that we all grow. Yes, we need to grow and look more like Christ now than we did last year. We need to continue to look more like Christ when it comes to living a holy life, being led by the Holy Spirit, casting out demons, preaching the Gospel, healing the sick, etc. I believe that if we as believers start to understand what it means to be a disciple, if we see both ourselves and others around us as disciples of Jesus and understand that we must obey and look like Him, our lives would be forever changed.

As I have previously said, the Book of Acts is like a diary. I want to encourage you to sit down and start to write your own diary about your life with God. Write down what God is doing in your life and how He is using you. Then, look at your diary and ask yourself if it looks like the Book of Acts. If it does, I am so happy and excited that you are living this amazing life. If it does not look like the Book of Acts, I truly believe that if you continue to read this book and listen to the teachings in the video series, God will transform your life, and your diary will look more and more like the diary of Paul, Peter, John, James, and Ananias. Why? Well, as I have previously said, Jesus is the same yesterday, today, and forever, which means that the Holy Spirit is the same yesterday, today, and forever. This means that God wants to use you to spread His Kingdom like He used the early disciples. Isn't that amazing?

So I want to challenge you to write a diary about your life and see how it looks. If it doesn't look like what you see in the Bible, something isn't wrong with the Bible. No, that means something is wrong with your life. It is not the Bible that needs to change to match up with your life. It is you that needs to change. But the good news is that if your life does not yet look like what we read in the Book of Acts, you can do something about it.

THE NEW BIRTH

LESSON TWO

Welcome to **Lesson Two** in this **Kickstart Package**. In this lesson, we will look at what it means to be born again. This is a very important topic because we cannot live the life Jesus has called as to live as His disciples if we are not born again.

We will start off by looking at two Scriptures that lay an important foundation for believers. 1 Corinthians 15:3-4 (NKJV) states, *"For I delivered to you first of all that which I also received: that Christ died for our sins according to the Scriptures, and that He was buried, and that He rose again the third day according to the Scriptures"*. 2 Corinthians 5:21 (NKJV) states, *"For He made Him who knew no sin to be sin for us, that we might become the righteousness of God in Him"*. These two verses speak about the pillar of Christianity. They speak about the cross and how Jesus died on the cross for you and me so that we, through Jesus, can receive a new life. In Him, we can experience freedom from our sins and righteousness from God. This is crucial for us to understand, but it is not enough to just hear about it, dream about it, or read about it. We need to experience the new birth and righteousness from God.

It's NOT enough to:

You NEED to EXPERIENCE it!

LIFE WITH JESUS

The Gospel of Jesus is the Good News, and it is powerful, but it is life changing only for those who not only believe in it but who are also born again. John 3:3 (NKJV) states, *"Jesus answered and said to him, 'Most assuredly, I say to you, unless one is born again, he cannot see the kingdom of God.'"* Jesus spoke this to a man named Nicodemus, the teacher of Israel. He wasn't just "a" teacher. He was "the" teacher of Israel. He was a very intelligent Pharisee who knew the Word of God better than anyone else in Israel. However, he did not understand that Jesus was talking about a spiritual birth. So Nicodemus asked Jesus a question in John 3:4 (NKJV): "... *How can a man be born when he is old? Can he enter a second time into his mother's womb and be born?*". As we can see by his response, Nicodemus did not understand that Jesus was not talking about being physically born again. Jesus answers in verse 5, "... *'Most assuredly, I say to you, unless one is born of water and the Spirit, he cannot enter the kingdom of God.'*" We can see from Jesus' response, that to enter the Kingdom of God, we must be spiritually born again.

I want to make it very clear to you that believing in God or having faith in God is not enough. Satan and the demons believe in God, and they are not saved. There are many people who believe in God and think that is enough, but it is not. It is not enough that you go to church every Sunday, or that you grew up in a Christian family, or that you think you are a good person. No, none of this is enough. You need to be born again by being baptized in water and with the Holy Spirit, as Jesus is referring to in John 3:5. And when you get born again out of water and Spirit, your new life has begun. Yes, this is where your new life begins and where Jesus will begin to transform you.

I would now like to ask you a question. Where, in the Bible, do we see the early

It's NOT enough to:

You NEED to be BORN AGAIN!

church preach the Gospel, and where do we see how people got born again in response to hearing the Gospel? Do we find it in the 39 books in the Old Testament? No, we don't find it there. Why? It's because the Old Testament was written before the cross; therefore, we do not see the new birth that Jesus speaks about in John 3:5 in the Old Testament. So where do we find it? Do we find it in the four Gospels: Matthew, Mark, Luke, and John? Many people would say "yes" to this question because people often think that the Gospel is preached in the Gospels. But the answer is still no. We do not see the Gospel preached or how people responded to the Gospel in the four Gospels of the New Testament because, serving as a bridge between the time of the Old and New Testaments, it was still before the cross.

So what do we see in the four Gospels? We read how Jesus preached in Mark 1:15 (NIV) *"The time has come," he said. "The kingdom of God has come near. Repent and believe the good news!"* . So, in the Gospels, Jesus preached that the time was near and that people needed to repent and believe in the Gospel. But Jesus did not tell the people to repent, be baptized, and that they would receive the gift of the Holy Spirit. Why? Because He could not yet fulfill this at that time. Since Jesus was still here on earth, there was no baptism in the name of Jesus Christ and no baptism with the Holy Spirit because, once more, the time we read about in the four Gospels was before the cross. Jesus had not yet died on the cross and been buried, nor had he risen again, ascended into heaven, nor sent His Holy Spirit down to earth. And this is why He preached in Mark 1:15 (NIV), *"... The kingdom of God has come near. Repent and believe the good news!"* So during the time of the four Gospels, no one got baptized to Jesus Christ, nor did anyone receive the gift of the Holy Spirit and speak in tongues. No, this happened after the cross.

So, again, where in the Bible do we see the early church preach the Gospel, and where do we see how people got born again in response to hearing the Gospel? The answer is in the Book of Acts. We don't see this in the 21 letters because the letters were written to people who were already believers and did not need to hear the Gospel and be told that they needed to be born again. You can see to whom the letters were written by the way they start. The 21 letters often start with "To the church in..." or "To the believers in..." The people addressed in the letters were already born again believers who had repented, been baptized in water, and received the Holy Spirit. So the Book of Acts is the only Book in the Bible where we see how people like you and me hear the Gospel and, in response, get born again through repentance and baptism in water and with the Holy Spirit.

In Acts 2, after Jesus died on the cross and after the Holy Spirit was sent down to earth, we read how the early disciples were filled with the Holy Spirit and stood up in front of a crowd of people and preached the Gospel. In Acts 2:37 (NKJV), we see the whole picture come together: Now when they heard this, they were cut to the heart, and said to Peter and the rest of the apostles, *"Men and brethren, what shall we do?"*. We can see from this verse that they were preaching in a way that condemned people's hearts, and they asked Peter and the rest, *"... What shall we do?"* This is a really good and important question. What answer should we give people when they ask, "What shall we do to be saved?" or "What shall we do to be born again?" We can see how we should answer from the response Peter gave in Acts 2:38 (NKJV): *"... Repent, and let every one of you be baptized in the name of Jesus Christ for the remission of sins; and you shall receive the gift of the Holy Spirit."*

Jesus died on the cross, was buried, and rose again, and now we—you and I—need

 # REPENT

AND BE

 # BAPTIZED

EVERYONE OF YOU,
IN THE NAME OF JESUS CHRIST
FOR THE FORGIVENESS OF YOUR SINS
AND YOU SHALL RECEIVE THE GIFT OF THE

 # HOLY SPIRIT

to take up our cross and follow His example. We need to die like Jesus died. Yes, we need to die to our sins and to our "self." Then, like Jesus was buried, we need to be buried. We need to bury our old life, and this is achieved when we are baptized to Jesus Christ. Just like Jesus rose from the dead, we need to rise and live the new life, equipped with the power of the Holy Spirit. It is so amazing to witness a person get born again. Yes, it is beautiful to see someone recognize and turn away from their sins, die to themselves, bury their old life in baptism, and then receive the Holy Spirit.

I would like to show you more examples in the book of Acts where we see people repent, get baptized, and receive the Holy Spirit. One example is located in Acts 19. Here, we read how Paul went to Ephesus and met some believers there. In Acts 19:2 (NIV), he asked them, *"... Did you receive the Holy Spirit when you believed?"* Wow, this is such an important question, and it is still a question that we need to ask people today. When we meet people who believe in God, we need to ask them, like Paul, "Did you receive the Holy Spirit when you believed?" It is important to ask them this question because it is possible to have faith in God without ever receiving the Holy Spirit.

I would now like to ask you the same question. Did you receive the Holy Spirit when you believed? In Acts 19:2 (NIV), the people answered Paul by saying, *"We have not so much as heard whether there is a Holy Spirit."* When Paul heard that the people in Ephesus had not received the Holy Spirit, he took the time to explain the Gospel to them. Later, we read in Acts 19:5-6 (NKJV), *"When they heard this, they were baptized in the name of the Lord Jesus. And when Paul had laid hands on them, the Holy Spirit came upon them, and they spoke with tongues and prophesied."* Hallelujah! This is what we need to do today. When I read the response they gave Paul, it makes me think of myself many years ago. I would have given an answer similar to theirs. I was a Christian, or at least I thought I was because I grew up in the Lutheran church, and I was baptized as a baby and later confirmed. Sure, I had faith in God, but I had not received the Holy Spirit. I was not born again, and I still needed to understand the full Gospel. I needed someone to come and help me understand that I needed to repent, to baptize me in water, and to pray for me to receive the Holy Spirit.

Today, I see what we read in Acts 19 happen all over the world. I have met so many people who believed in God, but when I ask them if they received the Holy Spirit when they believed, many of them say, "No, I haven't." If they haven't received the Holy Spirit, we need to take the time to share the Gospel with them. And when they repent and want to be baptized in water and with the Holy Spirit, help them with this. Baptize them in water. Lay hands on them, and pray for them to receive the Holy Spirit. It is so powerful and beautiful. Jesus is the same yesterday, today, and forever, and the Holy Spirit is the same yesterday, today, and forever. You can be born again today. You can get baptized to Christ and receive the Holy Spirit today, just like we read in Acts 2, Acts 19, and many other places throughout the book of Acts.

I would now like to draw your attention to Acts 10. Here, we read about how Peter visited a man named Cornelius. When he arrived at his house, we read how, when Peter was speaking to them, the Holy Spirit came over Cornelius and his whole family and they spoke in tongues. We see this in Acts 10:46-48 (NKJV), which states, *For they heard them speak with tongues and magnify God. Then Peter answered, "Can anyone forbid water, that these should not be baptized who have received the Holy Spirit just as we have?" And he commanded them to be baptized in the name of the Lord. Then they asked him to stay a few days.*

Wow, I love this verse because this is not something that we read about that only happened during that time. No, we see this happen day after day in many places all around the world. Sometimes, we see people repent and receive the Holy Spirit first, and then get baptized in water. Other times, we see people repent, get baptized in water first, and then receive the Holy Spirit. Though the order may vary slightly, it is important that you experience a true repentance. Then after you repent, get baptized in water and with the Holy Spirit.

Today, the problem is religion. Many of us grew up in religion and tradition. As I have said previously, I grew up in a Lutheran church. I did not attend the Lutheran church a lot, but being a part of the Lutheran church was the tradition in Denmark. I was told by the priest in the Lutheran church that we all have the Holy Spirit. Why? Because we were all baptized as a baby. But that was a lie. What my family and I grew up in, and what we got taught, was not the full Gospel. What we got taught was wrong. I was deceived for many years, but when I finally understood the full Gospel, repented, got baptized, and received the Holy Spirit, my life was changed forever, and I experienced freedom from my sin. But it took me six years to reach this freedom. Yes, it took me six years from the time I came to faith and repented to get baptized in water and with the Holy Spirit. Why? Well, because there was no one around me to explain the full Gospel to me and help me with these steps. So when I came to faith and repented, it took me six years until I got baptized in water and with the Holy Spirit. But it does not have to take such a long time for you. Paul, in Romans 1:16 (NKJV), says, *For I am not ashamed of the gospel of Christ, for it is the power of God to salvation for everyone who believes, for the Jew first and also for the Greek.* Yes, the Gospel is the power for everyone who believes. It has the power to transform a person from the inside out. Just like it has transformed many people living in the time of the Bible and many people living today, it can also transform your life.

So, let us review. There are three things that Peter spoke about in the Book of Acts that come together with having faith in Jesus. What are they? They are repentance, baptism in water, and baptism with the Holy Spirit. Acts 2:38 (NKJV) states, *Repent, and let every one of you be baptized in the name of Jesus Christ for the remission of sins; and you shall receive the gift of the Holy Spirit.* This is what we need to do today.

Repentance is more than just deciding to believe in Jesus. Repentance has to do with sin and deciding to turn away from sin. It is when you feel sorry for what you have done and choose to turn away and change your life. Colossians 3:5-10 (NIV) states:

Put to death, therefore, whatever belongs to your earthly nature: sexual immorality, impurity, lust, evil desires and greed, which is idolatry. Because of these, the wrath of God is coming. You used to walk in these ways, in the life you once lived. But now you must also rid yourselves of all such things as these: anger, rage, malice, slander, and filthy language from your lips. Do not lie to each other, since you have taken off your old self with its practices and have put on the new self, which is being renewed in knowledge in the image of its Creator.

Wow, this is amazing. What we read here perfectly describes repentance. Yes, repentance involves burying our old life and putting on the new life. It is when we see our sin and all of the things that we have done that are not pleasing to God and choose to turn away from all of it. It is when we realize that we have been living our own life and decide that we don't want that life anymore and make the decision to turn away from it. Repentance involves changing our hearts when it comes to sin and hating sin as God hates it. And when we repent and turn away from our sins, God will do something amazing. He will remove our stony hearts and give us new hearts of flesh, and He will write the law on our hearts.

I still remember when I believed and decided to repent. I remember how much I changed and how my conscience became like new. While growing up, there were things that I had always done and that I had always loved to do, and at the time, I did not feel like what I was doing was wrong because I was so used to doing it. But when I finally saw my sin and turned away from it, I received a new conscience, and I could no longer do what I did before. I could no longer continue living in sin. Why? Well, because those things I used to do belonged to my old life. They were not a part of me anymore. And When God gave me a new heart, I really wanted to please God and live the new life He gave me. 1 John 3:5-6 (NIV) states,

"But you know that he appeared so that he might take away our sins. And in him is no sin. No one who lives in him keeps on sinning. No one who continues to sin has either seen him or known him."

Wow, these are very radical words. They tell us that when we abide in Him, and when we know Him, we cannot continue sinning. Why? It is because He gave us a new heart. The next verse, 1 John 3:7-9, states:

"Dear children, do not let anyone lead you astray. The one who does what is right is righteous, just as he is righteous. The one who does what is sinful is of the devil, because the devil has been sinning from the beginning. The reason the Son of God appeared was to destroy the devil's work. No one who is born of God will continue to sin, because God's seed remains in them; they cannot go on sinning, because they have been born of God."

Again, wow, what we read here is so real. It is the truth, and we can experience this. You need to experience this new heart—God's seed inside of you—so that you cannot keep sinning the way you did before.

I want to tell you that, especially in the beginning, you will fall and make mistakes because you need to learn how to live this new life. But there is a difference between learning to live this life and making mistakes versus continuing to sin willfully. To sin willfully means to know it is sin and to make the conscious decision to do it anyway. Everyone who is truly born again and who has the seed of God inside cannot continue to sin willfully. When you fall as a newborn believer, you must rise again and then obey 1 John 1:9 (NIV), which states *"If we confess our sins, he is faithful and just and will forgive us our sins and purify us from all unrighteousness"*. Yes,

He is faithful and righteous, and He will forgive you when you ask for forgiveness.

I am sure that some of you know what I mean when I say that when you repent and put your faith in Jesus, God will give you a new heart and a new conscience and that you cannot continue living in sin. But if you do not know what I am talking about and have not experienced this, you are lost. Yes, if this is the case, you are lost right now, and you need to repent because when you truly repent and put your faith in God, you will experience this new heart and new conscience. So start with repentance, and then get baptized in water and with the Holy Spirit.

I now want to look at baptism in more detail. The word "baptize" (*Baptizó*) means "to dip" or "to immerse." To be baptized means to be dipped or immersed underwater. It represents the death and burial of the body. It is not, as some churches believe, a sprinkling of water. Jesus and the early disciples baptized people with full immersion in water. But how did the church come to accept a sprinkling of water as the way to be baptized? Well, the first time we see baptism done through sprinkling water was in the year 253 AD. It was permitted by a local bishop for a few special cases. In 753 AD, we saw the sprinkling of water become a form of baptism that was officially approved, but only for a few cases where there was no other option, like if people were lying in bed, sick, and could not get baptized with full immersion. In 1311 AD, the council of Ravenna declared that the sprinkling of water was the official way of baptizing people. I want to tell you that just because a bishop of a council said that it is okay to get baptized with a sprinkling of water, it does not mean that it is okay. We need to build on what the Bible says and not on a tradition.

Over the years, there have been many traditions that have crept into the church, and they are not biblical. One example of this is baby baptism. Here is a picture of me as a baby being baptized in the Lutheran church. As you can see, they put me in a white dress. If someone would try to put a white dress on me today, I would say, "NO WAY!" But at the time, I did not protest about wearing a white dress because I was a baby, and I did not care. I did not even understand what was going on. And even if I had been baptized naked, I would not have complained. Why? Well, because I was not aware of sin. I was only a baby. When Adam and Eve walked around in the garden before sin came and opened their eyes, they were not ashamed. They were not ashamed that they were naked because they did not see their nakedness. But when they ate from Tree of the Knowledge of Good and Evil, their eyes were opened, and they saw their nakedness. Yes, they felt ashamed, and they desperately wanted to cover themselves. In the same way that Adam and Eve were once unaware of sin, babies are also unaware of sin. So it is crazy to baptize babies! The early church did not baptize babies. No, you cannot find baby baptisms anywhere in the Bible. Baby baptisms were a tradition that came hundreds of years later. Suddenly, 500 years after Jesus walked on earth, someone had the idea to baptize babies and decided that it should be the new norm. But this is tradition, and it cannot save you. Only Jesus can save you.

So what is baptism? Is baptism just a symbol? No. It is also a tradition to call baptism a symbol. But baptism is not a symbol. Jesus states in Mark 16:16 (NKJV), *" He who believes and is baptized will be saved; but he who does not believe will be condemned"* . So Jesus said that the one who believes and is baptized would be saved. And what did the early disciples say in the book of Acts? In Acts 2:38 (NIV), Peter was preaching the Gospel, and people asked what they should do. Peter replied, *"Repent and be baptized, every one of you, in the name of Jesus Christ for the forgiveness of your sins. And you will receive the gift of the Holy Spirit"*. When Ananias baptized Paul in Acts 22:16 (NIV), he said to Paul, *"And now what are you waiting for? Get up, be baptized and wash your sins away, calling on his name."* So we see the early disciples in the book of Acts say that baptism is for the forgiveness of sins and also that it washes away sins. Does this sound like a symbol? No. How can we read what the Bible says about baptism and conclude that it is only a symbol?

What do the letters in the Bible say about Baptism? Romans 6:4 (NIV) says that,

through baptism, we die with Christ and rise with Christ by saying, *We were therefore buried with him through baptism into death in order that, just as Christ was raised from the dead through the glory of the Father, we too may live a new life.* 1 Corinthians 12:13 (NIV) says that, through baptism, we are baptized into one body by stating, *"For we were all baptized by one Spirit so as to form one body—whether Jews or Gentiles, slave or free—and we were all given the one Spirit to drink"*. Galatians 3:27 (NIV) explains that, through baptism, we put on Christ. It says, *for all of you who were baptized into Christ have clothed yourselves with Christ*. Colossians 2:12 (NIV) tells us that baptism is a circumcision of Christ and that we are buried with Christ. It states, ... *having been buried with him in baptism, in which you were also raised with him through your faith in the working of God, who raised him from the dead.* Titus 3:5 (NIV) tells us that baptism is a washing of rebirth by saying, *he saved us, not because of righteous things we had done, but because of his mercy. He saved us through the washing of rebirth and renewal by the Holy Spirit.* 1 Peter 3:21(NIV) says that baptism saves you: ... *and this water symbolizes baptism that now saves you also—not the removal of dirt from the body but the pledge of a clear conscience toward God. It saves you by the resurrection of Jesus Christ...".* Does baptism sound like a symbol? Of course, not!

The early disciples were very radical when it came to baptism, and we can see this in the way people responded to hearing how they preached the Gospel. In the Bible, when people came to faith, did they get baptized on the first Sunday after they came to faith? No. Did they get baptized, years after hearing the Gospel, when other people felt like they were ready to get baptized? No. In the Bible, when people heard the Gospel and came to faith, they got baptized right away. We can see this in Acts 2, where we read about 3,000 people who got baptized on the same day they came to faith. We also see this in Acts 10, where Peter visited Cornelius and his family. Here, we see Cornelius and his family get baptized with the Holy Spirit, and in response, Peter says in Acts 10:47-48 (NIV), *"Surely no one can stand in the way of their being baptized with water. They have received the Holy Spirit just as we have. So he ordered that they be baptized in the name of Jesus Christ ...".* So, as we can see, Cornelius and his family were baptized in water right away. We see another example in Acts 16, where the jailer and his household heard the Gospel and got baptized in the middle of the night. Why did we see so many people in the book of Acts get baptized right away after coming to faith? This is because baptism was the beginning of the new life. Yes, it was the beginning of a new life where they put off the old man and washed away their sins.

In baptism, the old life, under the bondage of sin, is buried and we are set free to live a new life. A very good illustration of baptism in the Old Testament is shown through Moses and the Israelites. The Old Testament is full of shadows and pictures of what will be fulfilled in the New Testament. In the Old Testament, we read about how the Israelites were slaves in Egypt under a ruler named Pharaoh. One day, Moses (a picture of Christ) went to Pharaoh and said, in Exodus 5:1, "... Let my people go..." But Pharaoh did not want to let the Israelites go. God then sent a series of plagues to Egypt so that Pharaoh would let the Israelites go. And in the end, God did something amazing. God sent an angel of death to kill all of the Egyptians' firstborn sons, and He told Moses to tell the Israelites to put the blood of a lamb over the door of their houses so that the angel of death would pass over their houses. So God saved the Israelites by the blood. This serves as a picture of Christ, as He is God's first-born son and His blood was poured out on the cross to save us from our sins. After this last plague, Pharaoh let the Israelites go and, at last, the Israelites were saved out of Egypt. When they came out of Egypt, they were rejoicing because they were saved by the blood. But they were still captives/slaves to their old life, so they still needed to bury their old life that was following them out of Egypt. Yes, they needed to find a way to be free from their old life of sin.

So how did the Israelites bury their old life of sin? Well, what happened next is amazing. Pharaoh regretted letting the Israelites go, so he sent his army after them. Suddenly, the Israelites went from rejoicing about their freedom to thinking that they were going to die. Yes, the Egyptians (their old life) were coming after them. So they needed to be saved one more time to fully escape and be free. God parted the Red Sea for the Israelites to cross over to the other side, and as they went across, the Egyptians (their old life) followed them. When the Israelites reached the other side, God closed the waters and drowned all of the Egyptians, and the Israelites were saved once and for all. They were no longer in chains, and they were not afraid that their old life would come and take them captive. But this was still not enough. They needed to continue their new life by being led by the cloud. Yes, they needed to walk by the Spirit to enter the Promised Land that God had prepared for them. And this is a picture of our salvation. We get saved from the world when we repent, and we get saved from our old life of sin through baptism in water. We then need to receive the Holy Spirit, and learn how to walk by the Spirit. And the one who continues to the end shall, one day, be saved. This is so beautiful, and this is what we need to experience today. If we continue reading Romans 6:3-7 (NIV), it states:

"Or don't you know that all of us who were baptized into Christ Jesus were baptized into his death? We were therefore buried with him through baptism into death in order that, just as Christ was raised from the dead through the glory of the Father, we too may live a new life. For if we have been united with him in a death like his, we will certainly also be united with him in a resurrection like his. For we know that our old self was crucified with him so that the body ruled by sin might be done away with, that we should no longer be slaves to sin—because anyone who has died has been set free from sin."

Hallelujah! This is so beautiful. This is what happens when we are baptized.

I still remember the day I read Romans 6:14 (NKJV), which states, *"For sin shall not have dominion over you, for you are not under law but under grace"* . This verse changed my life. At the time, I was still struggling with sin, and I was not free. I was just baptized, but baptism did not give me freedom. I did not understand it. But when I read Romans 6:14, I had a revelation about what baptism was, and I experienced a freedom from sin that I had never experienced before. On that day, I got truly born again. Today, I am not a slave to sin, and my life looks so different from what it did before. I am not saying that we won't make mistakes, but when we do, we know that we can ask for forgiveness and that He will forgive us.

If you are still a slave to sin, there can be different reasons for this. One reason for this is that you have not fully repented and turned away from your sins, or if you have turned away, that you were not baptized correctly. In order to be baptized correctly, you must first turn away from your sins and get a new heart before you can bury the old life. Many people grow up in a church, and get baptized as teenagers. But they come to understand what repentance is and turn away from their sins ten or fifteen years later. If you only turn away from sin after your baptism, then it was not a true baptism. There has been no repentance prior to baptism. You need to recognize your sins and turn away from them before you bury your old life. This is a big reason why you and many other people could be struggling with sin. Another reason is that, like me, you did not understand the power of baptism when you got baptized. It could be that you need to receive the power of baptism in faith. Read Romans 6, and ask God to open your eyes so that you can understand what happened to you when you got baptized, and so that you can live this new life. It is so important that you experience the new birth through repentance, and that you are saved from the old life through baptism and receiving the Holy Spirit.

QUESTIONS & ANSWERS

UNDERSTANDING THE BOOK OF ACTS

As you have seen in Lesson Two, I have been quoting different verses from the Book of Acts to show you what the early disciples preached and what people needed to do to be born again. Today, some people don't think of the Book of Acts as a theological book, as they believe that it is strictly a historical book. Some people believe that it is only a book that explains the past, and therefore, they think that we cannot draw theology from it like we can with the rest of the New Testament. But this argument is not valid because we see a lot of theology within the Book of Acts through what the early disciples said and did. Yes, you can see what the early disciples believed by how they lived. And we can, furthermore, see a confirmation of what they believed through reading the letters written to the different churches. The Book of Acts is a unique book, as it is not written like the letters in the Bible, nor is it written strictly like a theological book. It is a book that describes events that happened over 30 years. Sometimes it retells the specific details of events, and other times, it retells events vaguely.

I have heard people say that it is not necessary to be baptized because we do not see people get baptized every time someone comes to faith in the Book of Acts. It is true that, in some places in Acts, we do not read about baptism. One example of this is in Acts 6:7 (NKJV) , which states, *"Then the word of God spread, and the number of the disciples multiplied greatly in Jerusalem, and a great many of the priests were obedient to the faith"*. We don't read that the people got baptized in water, and we also don't read that they received the Holy Spirit. But you also need to realize that we don't read that they repented. We just read that the number of disciples grew and that they were obedient to the faith. But to be obedient to the faith means to obey Jesus in what He told us to do. So even if we don't read that they repented, got baptized in water, and received the Holy Spirit in Acts 6:7, it does not mean that it did not happen.

Even if repentance, baptism in water, and baptism with the Holy Spirit it is not recorded every time people came to faith throughout the Book of Acts, it does not mean that they do these things. Another clear example of this is Acts 9:35 (NKJV), which states, *"So all who dwelt at Lydda and Sharon saw him and turned to the Lord"*. Here, we read nothing about how they believed, repented, or got baptized in water

As you have seen in Lesson Two, I have been quoting different verses from the Book of Acts to show you what the early disciples preached and what people needed to do to be born again. Today, some people don't think of the Book of Acts as a theological book, as they believe that it is strictly a historical book. Some people believe that it is only a book that explains the past, and therefore, they think that we cannot draw theology from it like we can with the rest of the New Testament. But this argument is not valid because we see a lot of theology within the Book of Acts through what the early disciples said and did. Yes, you can see what the early disciples believed by how they lived. And we can, furthermore, see a confirmation of what they believed through reading the letters written to the different churches. The Book of Acts is a unique book, as it is not written like the letters in the Bible, nor is it written strictly like a theological book. It is a book that describes events that happened over 30 years. Sometimes it retells the specific details of events, and other times, it retells events vaguely.

I have heard people say that it is not necessary to be baptized because we do not see people get baptized every time someone comes to faith in the Book of Acts. It is true that, in some places in Acts, we do not read about baptism. One example of this is in Acts 6:7 (NKJV) , which states, *"Then the word of God spread, and the number of the disciples multiplied greatly in Jerusalem, and a great many of the priests were obedient to the faith"*. We don't read that the people got baptized in water, and we also don't read that they received the Holy Spirit. But you also need to realize that we don't read that they repented. We just read that the number of disciples grew and that they were obedient to the faith. But to be obedient to the faith means to obey Jesus in what He told us to do. So even if we don't read that they repented, got baptized in water, and received the Holy Spirit in Acts 6:7, it does not mean that it did not happen.

Even if repentance, baptism in water, and baptism with the Holy Spirit it is not recorded every time people came to faith throughout the Book of Acts, it does not mean that they do these things. Another clear example of this is Acts 9:35 (NKJV), which states, *"So all who dwelt at Lydda and Sharon saw him and turned to the Lord"*. Here, we read nothing about how they believed, repented, or got baptized in water or with the Holy Spirit. Does that mean that those people did not believe when they turned to the Lord, or that they did not get baptized when they turned to the Lord?

No, it just means that they did not include every detail because this is a historical book and not a theological book.

To fully understand the Book of Acts, it is important to "zoom-out." Yes, you need to look at the whole Book of Acts, from the beginning to the end, and not build your theology off of one verse or chapter in the Bible. When we do this, we will also see more information about what happened when people came to faith. There are many places in the Book of Acts where, instead of only reading that people turned to the Lord or believed, we read more about how people came to faith and got born again. For example, we see more detail in Acts 2, 8, 10, 16, and 19.

In Acts 2, we read how they preached repentance, baptism in water, baptism with the Holy Spirit, and how 3,000 people came to faith and were all baptized on the same day. In Acts 8, Philip traveled to Samaria, and in this chapter, you can clearly see that it is possible to be baptized in water without receiving the Holy Spirit. You can also read how Philip shared the Gospel with the eunuch and, in Acts 8:38, how the eunuch got baptized immediately after hearing the Gospel. Yes, baptism, from the verses in Acts that give us more detail, was the response we see he and everyone else had after hearing the Gospel. Acts 10 speaks about how Peter traveled to the house of Cornelius, and here, we see how the baptism with the Holy Spirit sometimes comes before baptism in water. We see this in Acts 10:44-48 (NKJV), which states:

While Peter was still speaking these words, the Holy Spirit fell upon all those who heard the word. And those of the circumcision who believed were astonished, as many as came with Peter, because the gift of the Holy Spirit had been poured out on the Gentiles also. For they heard them speak with tongues and magnify God. Then Peter answered, "Can anyone forbid water, that these should not be baptized who have received the Holy Spirit just as we have?" And he commanded them to be baptized in the name of the Lord. Then they asked him to stay a few days.

Again, Acts 16 provides in-depth detail as it speaks about how Paul and Silas were imprisoned and how the jailer there came to faith and immediately got baptized in the middle of the night. Acts 16:26-34 (NKJV) states:

Suddenly there was a great earthquake, so that the foundations of the prison were shaken; and immediately all the doors were opened and everyone's chains were loosed. And the keeper of the prison, awaking from sleep and seeing the prison doors open, supposing the prisoners had fled, drew his sword and was about to kill himself. But Paul called with a loud voice, saying, "Do yourself no harm, for we are all here." Then he called for a light, ran in, and fell down trembling before Paul and Silas. And he brought them out and said, "Sirs, what must I do to be saved?" So they said, "Believe on the Lord Jesus Christ, and you will be saved, you and your household." Then they spoke the word of the Lord to him and to all who were in his house. And he took them the same hour of the night and washed their stripes. And immediately he and all his family were baptized. Now when he had brought them into his house, he set food before them; and he rejoiced, having believed in God with all his household.

Finally, Acts 19 provides detail about Paul traveling to the believers in Ephesus. In Acts 19, Paul asked if they received the Holy Spirit, and when he found out that they had not, he shared the full gospel with them. After he prayed for them, they got baptized in water and with the Holy Spirit. We see this in Acts 19:6 (NKJV), which states, *"And when Paul had laid hands on them, the Holy Spirit came upon them, and they spoke with tongues and prophesied"*.

If we take these chapters mentioned above and put them together with the rest of the Book of Acts, we would see a very clear picture how people repented, got baptized, and received the Holy Spirit when they came to faith. We do not read anything about a sinner's prayer or asking Jesus into your heart, which many people do today instead of what we read here in the Book of Acts.

Do not be deceived by people who argue against baptism in water or with the Holy Spirit by saying there are places in the Bible where you do not see people get baptized after they came to faith. Just because it is not always recorded, it does not mean that it didn't happen. It is the same with repentance. In some verses in Acts, as I have shown you, we do not read that the people repented when they came to faith, but again, just because we don't read about it in some of the Scriptures, it does not mean that they didn't repent. When we "zoom out" and take a look at the whole Book of Acts, we can see that what is preached in Acts 2:38 (repentance, baptism in water and with the Holy Spirit) is the message of the Gospel that continued throughout the entire book.

Something very important to understand about the Bible is that it was originally written without chapters and verses. Chapters and verses were added much later. A Jewish rabbi named Nathan divided the Old Testament into verses in A.D. 1488 and in 1555, a man named Robert Estienne, otherwise known as Stephanus, divided the New Testament into numbered verses. So we must realize that it is important to read a whole book in the Bible before we are able to understand the context and message of that book. Yes, reading only one or two chapters at a time was not how the Bible was originally designed to be read. We must remember to look at the whole book to truly understand the message.

REPENTANCE IS THROUGHOUT OUR WHOLE LIFE

Repentance is not only something that happens once in your life, but it is something that happens throughout your whole life, and it is very important to understand this. Throughout Lesson Two, when I am referring to repentance, I am referring to the very first time you repent and believe and the moment God gives you the new heart. Yes, I am talking about the moment you recognize and turn away from your sin, turn to God, and receive a new heart. I am talking about the moment God takes out your stone heart and gives you a heart of flesh on which He writes his law. Most people can name the date or time when they experienced this first repentance. But, aside from this, repentance is something that we continue doing throughout our whole life.

Repentance is something that continually goes deeper and deeper. Today, I still repent, but the things I repent of now are very different compared to when I first repented. When a person first repents and gets a new heart, the first sign that they have done this is often how they speak. They often immediately change their language. Jesus says, in Luke 6:45 (NKJV), *"A good man out of the good treasure of his heart brings forth good; and an evil man out of the evil treasure of his heart brings forth evil. For out of the abundance of the heart his mouth speaks"*. So Jesus says that out of the mouth will flow what is in the heart.

Before I first repented, my heart was full of evil and blasphemous things, and it naturally flowed out of my mouth. But when I repented and received a new heart of flesh, I did not want to say those evil things anymore. It was like I couldn't. I started to ask myself, "Torben, why do you speak in this way? Why do you curse? Why do you blaspheme God?" I started to reflect on the way I spoke because my heart was changed, and I could no longer continue speaking out evil and blasphemous things. It was like it tasted wrong in my mouth.

After a person changes the way they speak, they will continue to change the more concrete things in their lives. For example, before I repented, I had a girlfriend, and we slept together. At the time, I didn't think it was wrong. And when I repented and received a new heart, it still took me some time to learn to obey Jesus and discern sin, and so, again, I slept with her. But after I repented, when I did this, I felt so guilty and ashamed. It was like an alarm went off in my head, and all I could think was, "SIN, SIN, SIN!" I knew that I could not continue living in sin with her, so I ended our relationship.

When a person repents and receives a new heart, they are still surrounded by sin. For me, I was still around my friends, drinking, and so on. But, like me, someone who has repented and received a new heart, cannot continue living a sinful lifestyle. And even if this person sins once or twice more, they will feel inside of them that they cannot continue sinning anymore. They will feel that it is wrong. Over time, God will completely change this person, and it will be clear for everyone around them to see that they have repented.

Today, I still repent, but it is no longer of concrete things like drinking, cursing, or falling into sexual sin like in the beginning. No, those sins are far away from me, and it should be like this for everyone who has been working for the Lord for a long time. Now my repentance has to do with more internal things, like the motives of my heart. I have to analyze myself and ask, "Am I proud? Did I say something wrong? Did I hurt someone with my words? Do I have any unforgiveness in my heart?" So I still repent, but today, it is on a much deeper level than it was in the beginning. This is crucial to explain to people who have just repented and come to faith. Yes, tell them that they now have a new heart, but it doesn't mean that life will be easy. Tell them that they need to be ready to repent if they do something wrong and that they need to let God work in their lives to produce holiness and, in the end, eternal life. Again, when we ask people if they have repented, we are asking them if they have turned away from their sins and received the new heart the Bible talks about. And for us "older" disciples, we should keep in repentance, be careful not to allow sin to enter into our life, and continue to let God work in us.

DON'T TWIST THE SCRIPTURES

I know that baptism, for many people, is very difficult because of our traditions. When it comes to baptism, I can see how the enemy has tried to put fear into people and how he has tried to make it an uncomfortable topic so that people won't talk about it or ask questions about it. But, as we can see in the Bible, it is very important to talk about it. We cannot just ignore what Jesus says about it.

Jesus, in Mark 16:16 (NKJV), states, *"He who believes and is baptized will be saved; but he who does not believe will be condemned"*. Many people try to twist Jesus' words here and say that we don't need to be baptized because Jesus said that those who don't believe shall be condemned. He did not say those who do not believe and are not baptized shall be condemned. But this argument is foolish and without merit because Jesus did not need to say that the one who does not believe and is not baptized shall be condemned because if you don't believe, then you will also not be baptized. It is already clear, and therefore, there is no need to repeat it.

I have heard many different arguments against baptism. Acts 2:38 (NKJV) states, *"Then Peter said to them, 'Repent, and let every one of you be baptized in the name of Jesus Christ for the remission of sins; and you shall receive the gift of the Holy Spirit' "*. Some people read this verse and think that when people believe, they are automatically immersed because Peter does not mention immersion in water. Therefore, they do not believe that Peter is talking about baptism in water. But arguments like this are not logical because if we, again, "zoom out" and look at the whole Book of Acts, we can see many examples where it is clear that baptisms took place in water. For example, we can see that Philip, in Acts 8, baptized the eunuch in water, or that John the Baptist, in John 3, baptized people in the Jordan because there was much water there. Arguments like this, which try to remove the water from baptism by saying that baptism just means to be immersed and that we are immersed into Jesus when we believe, are perfect examples of twisting the Word of God, and I could come up with many more examples like this.

So if you struggle with baptism or any other subject in the Bible, then as I have said, "zoom out." Try, for example, to look at the Book of Acts and the whole New Testament from the beginning to the end. And when you do this and set aside your traditions, you will find that things will become clear, and you will see that baptism is simple and very powerful.

PHYSICAL AND SPIRITUAL

Today, the world, and especially the church, has divided the physical things from the spiritual things. But this is not a biblical, nor a Hebrew way of thinking. No, it is a Greek way of thinking. In fact, the Hebrew way of thinking is to believe that the physical and spiritual world are very connected. For example, located in the Garden of Eden were physical trees called the Tree of Knowledge of Good and Evil and the Tree of Life. When Adam and Eve ate from the Tree of Life, they should live forever, but when they ate from the Tree of Knowledge of Good and Evil, they would die. So here, eating from the physical trees had a spiritual consequence. Another example of the physical and spiritual world being connected is found in 2 Kings 5, where it speaks about a man named Naaman. Naaman suffered from leprosy, and the prophet, Elisha, told him to go and dip himself in the Jordan River seven times and that he would be healed. When Naaman obeyed God and did this, God used the water to completely heal him. So the physical water had a spiritual impact, and Naaman was physically healed. Communion is also physically and spiritually connected, and we can see this from what Paul says in 1 Corinthians 27-30 (NKJV), which states:

Therefore whoever eats this bread or drinks this cup of the Lord in an unworthy manner will be guilty of the body and blood of the Lord. But let a man examine himself, and so let him eat of the bread and drink of the cup. For he who eats and drinks in an unworthy manner eats and drinks judgment to himself, not discerning the Lord's body. For this reason many are weak and sick among you, and many sleep.

It is also the same with baptism. In baptism, you are physically immersed in water, and it has a significant spiritual impact. Like God used the water to wash away Naamon's leprosy in the Old Testament, God, in the New Testament, uses the water to wash away peoples' sins. It is crucial to abandon the Greek way of thinking and to realize that the correct way to understand the Bible is to acknowledge that the physical world and spiritual world are in fact closely related and that one affects the other. We don't believe that the water is magical and special in any way. It is not the water, but the faith. Faith together with water is what God has chosen to use to wash away our sins and bury the old life.

FREE FROM SIN BUT NOT SINLESS

When I talk about how, in Christ, we can experience freedom from our sins, I am not talking about sinlessness. I am also not saying that we are slaves to sin because we are not. I have heard people in the church argue that we, as Jesus' followers, are not supposed to be free from sin because if we were, then we would not need Christ anymore, as we would be perfect and without sin. Firstly, I would like to say that we will always need Christ. It is only in Him that we can overcome our sin. Jesus did not die on the cross so that we could remain in sin. No, He died for us so that we could experience freedom from our sins. But this doesn't mean that we are sinless.

If someone told me that they had not sinned for the last 50 years, this person would either be blind or a liar because you cannot be sinless like this while we are still here on earth, waiting for the return of Jesus. Being free from our sins means that we don't need to go back to our old sins again and again. Yes, it means that we are free to choose to not go back and commit those same sins because we are no longer a slave to those sins. But if you make a mistake and do something *wrong, the Bible tells us that we can ask for forgiveness and that He will forgive us*. We see this in 1 John 1:9 (NKJV): *"If we confess our sins, He is faithful and just to forgive us our sins and to cleanse us from all unrighteousness"*.

When I first came to faith and repented, my heart changed, but I still did not feel free. I often felt condemned and bound by sin because I kept falling into the same sin again and again. And when I read Romans 7:14-20 (NKJV), I felt like it was talking about my life, for it states:

For we know that the law is spiritual, but I am carnal, sold under sin. For what I am doing, I do not understand. For what I will to do, that I do not practice; but what I hate, that I do. If, then, I do what I will not to do, I agree with the law that it is good. But now, it is no longer I who do it, but sin that dwells in me. For I know that in me (that is, in my flesh) nothing good dwells; for to will is present with me, but how to perform what is good I do not find. For the good that I will to do, I do not do; but the evil I will not to do, that I practice. Now if I do what I will not to do, it is no longer I who do it, but sin that dwells in me.

At that time, I believed that what I read in Romans 7:14-20 was the normal Christian life. But I later came to realize that Paul, in Romans 7, is speaking about someone who is bound to sin and that he is not describing the normal Christian life. The normal Christian life is described in Romans 6. Romans 6:6 (NKJV) states, *"... knowing this, that our old man was crucified with Him, that the body of sin might be done away with, that we should no longer be slaves of sin"*. Yes, it is a life of freedom from sin, where sin has no dominion over you.

When I first understood this freedom, it changed everything. I realized that I was free to not go back to the same sin again and again. I also realized that though we as believers are free, we are still not sinless. I sometimes still said something that I should not have said, thought something I should not have thought, or did something I should not have done. But when I did these things, I asked for forgiveness. God forgave me, and I moved on. So there is a big difference between being free from sin and being sinless.

To be free from sin means that when/if you do something wrong, you are free to turn away from it and change. Yes, it means that you don't need to continue living in it. You can move on! So, as believers, we are not sinners enslaved by sin. We are saints, free from sin. We can experience the Holy Spirit working in us and changing us to be more holy like our Father in heaven. It is a journey where we, especially in the beginning, will sometimes fall and make mistakes, but we don't need to, nor can we, continue to live a life of sin.

ONLY ONE BAPTISM

We believe in only one baptism; however, there are many people who get baptized again. But to those people who get baptized "again," this "second baptism" is something they should, from now on, look at as their first baptism and recognize that the other "baptism" they had before was not real. For example, I was "baptized" as a baby, but when I later came to faith and repented, I chose to get baptized "again." Some people might think that I was baptized twice, but I don't see it that way. To me, my baby "baptism" was not real, and therefore, the "second" baptism I did later in life was my first and only baptism.

It is important that the people who choose to get baptized "again" understand that the "baptism" they had before was not a real baptism. If they still saw it as real, then why would they get baptized again? So, if they choose to get baptized again after realizing that their first "baptism" was not real, it is important that, this time, they really understand what baptism is, that they repented, and that they acknowledge that this is the final and only baptism they will ever need. It is crucial that they recognize this because we don't want people to think that they should get re-baptized when they have a bad day or when they hear a good sermon. Yes, we want to avoid people getting baptized two, three, or four times. As we see in the Bible, there should only be one baptism, and hopefully, when the churches return to this understanding, we will not need to "re-baptize" people because people will have been baptized correctly the first time.

We often see people get baptized twice or three times because they have been in what we call "religion." Many people got baptized without really understanding what sin was and without true repentance. This is the reality, and when we go out and spread the Gospel and see the Kingdom of God grow, we will hear many people say this.

Every person's situation is different, and therefore, it is important to take the time to talk to everyone who wants to get baptized. We must talk to them about true repentance to make sure they fully understand what repentance is about and to make sure they are ready to repent. It is important for them to understand that, when they get baptized, it will be a new beginning for them and that it will be their only baptism. When you are confident that they understand these things, then you should baptize them.

When I say that there is only one baptism, I am referring to the baptism in the name of Jesus Christ. Before Jesus died on the cross, people were baptized, but it was not a baptism to Jesus. It was John's baptism of repentance. And those people who were baptized with John's baptism of repentance were later re-baptized into Christ. We can see this clearly in Acts 19:3-4 (NIV), where Paul met some disciples and asked them what baptism they received. As it states, *"So Paul asked, 'Then what baptism did you receive?' 'John's baptism,' they replied. Paul said, 'John's baptism was a baptism of repentance. He told the people to believe in the one coming after him, that is, in Jesus' "*. So Paul needed to explain the whole Gospel to them and how baptism is where we are buried with Christ and rise with Christ to receive a new life. And after they heard Paul's message, they were all baptized (again), but this time to Jesus Christ. But this situation in the Bible should not be an issue for us today because we don't meet people who were baptized with John's baptism and therefore need to be re-baptized to Christ. But we do, however, meet many people who were baptized in the name of religion and tradition and who have not fully repented. And when we meet these people, we need to explain the full Gospel to them and then, when they have repented, baptize them.

HOW DO I KNOW IF MY BAPTISM WAS CORRECT?

The truth is, we can baptize people incorrectly. We can "baptize" people and call it a "baptism," even when it's not. For example, when I was "baptized" as a baby in the Lutheran church, everyone accepted it as a baptism, even though, today, I recognize that it was not. Why? Well, it wasn't a real baptism because, as a baby, I did not recognize my sin, I did not repent, and the "baptism" was not with full immersion. Therefore, despite what people say, that was not a real baptism.

I have seen many people grow up in church and get baptized with full immersion, but I would regard some of them as incorrect as a Lutheran or Catholic baptism done with a sprinkling of water. Why? It is because, often times, the most important part that is necessary for a correct baptism is missing—repentance. Repentance needs to come before baptism, and not after. How can you bury your old life if you have not repented, turned away from your sins, and received a new heart from God? Therefore, if people get baptized without repentance, even with full immersion in water, I would compare it to taking a bath. They are not burying anything, since they have not crucified their flesh and old life. So repentance absolutely must come before baptism.

In this lesson, when I talk about repentance, I am, again, talking about the first time you recognize your sin, turn away from it, and receive a new heart. We will meet people who grew up in church who say, for example, that they got baptized in water when they were about 14 years old, but when they were around 30 years old, they finally saw their sins and repented and changed their life. A lot of them lived in sin before and after their "baptism," and there was no change in their life afterwards. Do they need to be baptized again? Yes, they do. Why? Because their repentance came after they were "baptized," and so it was not a real baptism.

So, this moment of repentance is very important, and it needs to happen before baptism. They need to experience that moment when they recognize their sins and can no longer enjoy sin and continue in sin like they did before. Why, when this moment of repentance comes, can't people continue to enjoy sin? It is because the seed of God was placed inside of them, and they can no longer live in sin.

It is very important when you baptize people that you take the time to listen to their life story. Listen to their testimony to see if it matches up with Scripture. And when you baptize them (again), make sure they understand that this baptism they are about to do is their only and final baptism, as we do not want people to get baptized again and again. There is only one baptism, and we can see this in Ephesians 4:4-5 (NIV), which states, *"There is one body and one Spirit, just as you were called to one hope when you were called; one Lord, one faith, one baptism..."*. But because of the traditions of man, we have unfortunately needed to baptize hundreds of people again. All of those people whom we baptized (again) recognized their sins and understood that their former "baptism" was not real and that the one they were about to do was their only real and final baptism.

WHY BAPTIZE PEOPLE IN THE NAME OF JESUS?

As you may have noticed throughout this lesson, when I talk about baptism, I talk about how people were baptized in the name of Jesus. I want to tell you that there is another wrong tradition in the church when it comes to baptism, and it is about the name we use to baptize people. Many people will argue that we should baptize in the name of the Father, Son, and the Holy Spirit, as Matthew 28:19 (NKJV) states, *"Go therefore and make disciples of all the nations, baptizing them in the name of the Father and of the Son and of the Holy Spirit…".* I also used to believe this, and I did this for many years, but then, one day, I started to look at what the disciples did in the Book of Acts, after Jesus went to heaven.

Take a moment to compare Matthew 28:19 (NKJV) where Jesus said to baptize people in the name of the Father, Son, and Holy Spirit to Acts 2:38, where Peter states, *"… Repent, and let every one of you be baptized in the name of Jesus Christ for the remission of sins; and you shall receive the gift of the Holy Spirit".* Here, Peter did not say to repent and be baptized in the name of the Father, Son, and Holy Spirit. He said to be baptized in the name of Jesus Christ. We can see how the name of Jesus was used to baptize people throughout the entire New Testament.

So, we know from what Peter said in Acts 2:38, that the 3,000 people who got baptized in Acts 2:41 were all baptized in the name of Jesus. We also see another example where people were baptized in the name of Jesus in Acts 8. Peter and John went to Samaria to pray for the believers there to receive the Holy Spirit, and in Acts 8:16 (NKJV), it is written, *"For as yet He had fallen upon none of them. They had only been baptized in the name of the Lord Jesus".* Ananias also baptized Paul in the name of Jesus and said to him, in Acts 22:16 (NKJV), *"And now why are you waiting? Arise and be baptized, and wash away your sins, calling on the name of the Lord".* So we can see in the Book of Acts that people got baptized in the name of either the "Lord Jesus," or "Jesus Christ" and never in the name of the Father, Son, and Holy Spirit.

We continue to see more examples of how people should be baptized in the name of Jesus in the letters. For example, in Romans 6:3 (NKJV), we read, *"Or do you not know that as many of us as were baptized into Christ Jesus were baptized into His death?".* We also see another example in Galatians 3:27 (NKJV): *"For as many of you as were baptized into Christ have put on Christ".* So when we look at the whole Bible, we can see many verses that talk about baptizing in the name of Jesus, but we don't actually find examples of people baptizing in the name of the Father, Son, and Holy Spirit.

So why did no one in the New Testament obey Jesus when He said to baptize people in the name of the Father, Son, and Holy Spirit? Well, there are two possible explanations for this. One explanation is that we have misunderstood what Jesus said in Matthew 28:19. Perhaps, Jesus, in Matthew 28:19, referred to the Father, Son, and the Holy Spirit because all three are part of baptism. Yes, maybe He was talking about how we need to repent to the Father, get baptized to the Son, Jesus Christ, and get filled with the Holy Spirit. And if this is what Jesus meant, then it makes sense that He would mention being baptized in the name of the Father, Son, and Holy Spirit because all three are part of the whole process of being born again. Yes, Jesus wants us to go out and tell people to repent to the Father, baptize people to the Son, and receive the Holy Spirit.

Another explanation focuses on the name of the Father, Son, and Holy Spirit. So what is the name of the Son? We know that it is "Jesus." But what is the name of the Father or the Holy Spirit? The Holy Spirit is often referred to as the "Spirit of Christ," the "Spirit of God," or the "Holy Spirit." This means that the Holy Spirit is part of God and the Son. And Jesus states in John 14:9, "... *He who has seen Me has seen the Father...*" indicating that Jesus and the Father are one. Acts 4:12 speaks of the name of Jesus when it says, *"Nor is there salvation in any other, for there is no other name under heaven given among men by which we must be saved"*. And Romans 10:13 (NKJV) states, *"For 'whoever calls on the name of the Lord shall be saved."* So it is clear that the name of Jesus is above every name, and it has the power to save. And because Matthew 28:19 is not saying that we should go out and baptize people in the names of the Father, Son, and Holy Spirit, but in the name, we can conclude that there is only one name for all three, and that is Jesus Christ.

Despite how you interpret Matthew 28:19, we should not build our understanding on one verse alone. We need to look at the whole New Testament to understand Matthew 28:19 and when we do this, we can clearly see that everyone got baptized to Christ. Why? Well, because it was Jesus who died on the cross, was buried, and rose from the grave. And in baptism, we are doing the same thing. Baptism is when we die with Christ, leaving behind our old life, and rise up with Him. This is shown in Romans 6:4 (NKJV), which states, *"Therefore we were buried with Him through baptism into death, that just as Christ was raised from the dead by the glory of the Father, even so we also should walk in newness of life"*. So it is important to baptize in the name of Jesus.

When I got baptized, I was baptized in the name of the Father, Son, and the Holy Spirit, and I have not gotten re-baptized. Why? Well, when I got baptized, I understood that I was being baptized to Christ, and I believe that God is greater than what the person baptizing you says. Even if the person who baptizes you says something wrong, it does not mean that your baptism is incorrect. But I also believe that when you understand that we should baptize in the name of Jesus and are disobedient to this, then I believe you are sinning. Yes, when we understand this truth, we have a responsibility to baptize in the name of Jesus. Therefore, now I always baptize people to Christ.

When I baptize people, I often ask them, "Are you ready to get baptized to Jesus?" When they reply, "Yes," I then say, "I baptize you to Christ." They then go down under the water, and as they do this, I say, "Die with Christ." As they are coming up out of the water, I say, "Rise with Christ." The Bible does not tell us what we need to specifically say when people get baptized, but we know that they need to be baptized in the name of Jesus.

There is power in the name of Jesus Christ. If you baptize people and say, "In the name of the Father, Son, and Holy Spirit," you are not saying the name above all names, the name of Jesus. When we pray for healing for the sick, we don't say, "Be healed in the name of the Father, Son, and the Holy Spirit." And we also don't cast out demons in the name of the Father, Son, and Holy Spirit. No, we pray for the sick and cast our demons in the name of Jesus. Why? This is because demons know that name, and there is so much power in that name. And we can see, in Matthew 28:18 (NKJV), that Jesus has all authority, as it states, *"And Jesus came and spoke to them, saying, "All authority has been given to Me in heaven and on earth"*.

So I encourage you to baptize people in the name of Jesus Christ. But if you meet people who have repented before they got baptized, but were baptized in the name of the Father, Son, and Holy Spirit, it is okay. I do not believe that they need to be baptized again. But now that you know the truth, baptize people in the name of Jesus, and you will see the power in His name.

NEVER COMPARE YOUR BAPTISM

You may have seen from our YouTube videos or movies that baptism is very powerful. In baptism, we have seen demons come out with loud screams, people get healed, and people shout out in new tongues. Yes, we have seen many amazing things through baptism. But I want to make something very clear to you. Never compare your baptism to anyone else's.

When I was baptized, there was no demonic manifestation. Why? Well, because I did not have any demons. I also already had the Holy Spirit and spoke in tongues when I got baptized, so I did not jump out of the water and start to speak in new tongues. So my baptism was peaceful, with no manifestations, and it changed my life forever. When I returned home after my baptism, I read Romans 6, and I received a revelation. Yes, I realized that I was free from sin, that my old life was buried, and that I was now free to walk in the newness of life that Christ called me to. But this revelation did not come the moment I was baptized.

Each person is different. Some people experience demonic manifestations and deliverance, and some people experience the Holy Spirit come in a powerful way and start shouting in new tongues. Other people will not experience anything the moment they are baptized, but that does not mean that their baptism is less than anyone else's. It is very important to never compare your baptism with others because each person is different, and how people experience baptism is different. No matter what the person experiences during baptism, if they have repented and decided to follow Jesus, it is a washing away of sins, a burial of the old life, and a new beginning.

HOW DO I BAPTIZE PEOPLE PRACTICALLY?

When you find people who have repented and want to be baptized, find some water to baptize them in. It can be a bathtub, a pool, a river, the sea, anywhere they can be fully immersed in water. Make sure, especially if it is a woman being baptized, that they are not wearing a white shirt, as it can become see-through when it gets wet. It is important to understand that everyone can baptize. It is not about being ordained or having a special position at a church. No, it is about following the call that Jesus has given us and making disciples.

When you baptize people, it doesn't matter if they want to go forward or backward into the water, but it is important that they are baptized with full immersion. They must also understand the full Gospel, recognize their sin, repent, and be ready to be baptized. Before we baptize people, we do a repentance talk with them. We do this to make sure that they have understood the Gospel. We ask them, "What sins do you want to wash away?" There is so much power in confessing sins to other people. No, they don't have to confess every sin they have ever committed in their entire life, but they may have certain sins that they want to confess to you. And when you ask them these questions, it may help them to fully realize that baptism and repentance go together and that they are washing away their sins. Then we ask them, "What do you want to bury in the water?" They may be carrying around the heavy weight of depression, fear, unforgiveness, hurt, and so on. It is important to ask them about this because baptism is not only about washing away sins, but also about burying the old life. And then we ask them, "Have you received the Holy Spirit?" And this is a very good question to ask because when they come out of the water, we need to know if we need to pray for them to receive the Holy Spirit and speak in tongues. During the baptism, if they have confessed some sins to you, try and keep it private if there are other people around so that you don't embarrass them.

When they are ready to be baptized, we get them into the water and ask them, "Are you ready to wash away your sins?" When they answer, "Yes," we then ask, "Are you ready to get baptized to Christ on your own faith?" And when they answer, "Yes," we say, "We baptize you to Jesus Christ." We then put them under the water, and as they go down, we say, "Die with Christ," and as they come out of the water, we say, "Rise with Christ." When they come out of the water, we take the time to pray for them, and this is very important for you to do. Thank God for washing away their sins, pray for freedom, and pray that all the shame and guilt of their sins would vanish. Pray that they would leave every sin behind in the water. You can also pray specifically for the things they confessed to you. For example, if they told you that they struggled with addiction, unforgiveness, depression, anxiety, or occult things, then you can pray for freedom from those things. You can say, for example, "I break all addiction in the name of Jesus, and I command any spirit of addiction to leave you" or, "I break all fear and depression, and I command every unclean spirit to leave you now, in the name of Jesus."

Since you bury your old life in baptism, demons have nothing to hold onto, and they have to go. Sometimes you will see demons start to manifest when people come out of the water. When this happens, don't be afraid. Just cast it out in the name of Jesus. Other times, when people come out of the water, you will see God start to heal their deep, painful wounds, and they may start to weep. No matter what you see them experience, take the time to pray for freedom for them. Once they are free, pray for them to receive the Holy Spirit if they don't have Him already. Encourage them to open their mouth and just speak out the first words. If they already have the Holy Spirit, encourage them to speak in tongues because it will flow deeper and more naturally from them since they have buried their old life and have washed away their sins.

I want to encourage you to not be afraid. Remember that we are disciples/apprentices and we learn by doing. Sometimes we will make mistakes. Sometimes you might feel like you did not explain the Gospel well enough, that you did not pray for them long enough, or maybe that you kept them in the cold water for too long. I encourage you to learn from your mistakes, and you will become better and better at ministering to people for God. So don't fear. Start to go out and obey Jesus' command to make disciples. If you need more inspiration, you can check out our YouTube videos and movies.

BORN OUT OF WATER AND SPIRIT

Jesus states in John 3:5-6 (NIV): *"Very truly I tell you, no one can enter the kingdom of God unless they are born of water and the Spirit. Flesh gives birth to flesh, but the Spirit gives birth to spirit"*. There is a lot of misunderstanding surrounding what Jesus said here. Some people today believe that when Jesus said you must be born of water that He was referring to the physical birth.

When a baby is born, it is born out of water from the mother's womb. But if Jesus had been referring to the physical birth, then He would have said something like this: "You cannot enter the Kingdom of God unless you are born out of the womb and the Spirit." But this interpretation to what Jesus said in John 3:5 makes no logical sense. Not only does it make no sense, it also takes away the power of baptism in water from the whole Gospel.

The people who believe that Jesus was referring to the physical birth here also believe that baptism in water is just a symbol and not necessary to be saved. These people often believe that once someone comes to faith and repents that they automatically receive the Holy Spirit. But they do not recognize the life-transforming power there is in baptism in water and with the baptism of the Holy Spirit.

So if Jesus was referring to the physical birth in John 3:5, He would be saying that no one can enter the Kingdom of God unless they are born from their mother's womb and the Spirit. But this is a foolish interpretation of John 3:5 because everyone who ever lived was born from their mother's womb. Yes, everyone Jesus spoke to, everyone who lived during Jesus' time here on earth, everyone who reads the Bible, everyone reading this book, and everyone in the entire world have all been born from their mother's womb. So it does not make logical sense that Jesus would tell people who are already born from their mother's womb that unless they were born from the womb, they cannot enter the Kingdom of God. If He were really referring to the physical birth, then He would simply have needed to say that unless you are born by the Spirit, you cannot enter into the Kingdom of God because they are already born from the womb, the physical birth.

Jesus was actually referring to the spiritual birth here in John 3:5-6 and not the physical birth. However, the physical birth paints a really good picture that we can use to understand the spiritual birth. For example, those who are born physically from the womb come from the darkness (of the womb) into the light (of the earth). This represents repentance. Then, the umbilical cord needs to be cut, and this is a picture of baptism in water, where people cut away their old life. Then, if the baby doesn't automatically take its first breath, the doctors/nurses will lay hands on the baby and do what is necessary to help the baby to breathe. This represents praying for people to receive the Holy Spirit. And when the baby takes its first breath, the baby will cry, and this represents speaking in new tongues. So when Jesus states in John 3:6 (NIV), *"Flesh gives birth to flesh, but the Spirit gives birth to spirit,"* He is referring to both the physical and the spiritual birth, and that it is important for all of us to be born spiritually.

THE HOLY SPIRIT

LESSON THREE

Welcome to **Lesson Three** in this **Kickstart Package**. In the last lesson, we looked at what it means to be born again, repentance, and baptism in water. In this lesson, we are going to look at the baptism with the Holy Spirit and speaking in tongues.

I would like to start off by quoting John 7:37-39 (NKJV), which states:

On the last day, that great day of the feast, Jesus stood and cried out, saying, "If anyone thirsts, let him come to Me and drink. He who believes in Me, as the Scripture has said, out of his heart will flow rivers of living water." But this He spoke concerning the Spirit, whom those believing in Him would receive; for the Holy Spirit was not yet given, because Jesus was not yet glorified.

Here, Jesus was speaking about the Holy Spirit. It is interesting that, in these verses, Jesus said the Holy Spirit had not yet been given to anyone because He had not yet been glorified. Yes, while Jesus walked on earth, He could only speak and teach about the Holy Spirit. He could not yet baptize anyone with the Spirit because He first needed to die on the cross, be buried, rise from the grave, and ascend into heaven before He could send His Holy Spirit down to earth.

Jesus continues to talk about the Holy Spirit in John 16:7, which states, *"Nevertheless I tell you the truth. It is to your advantage that I go away; for if I do not go away, the Helper will not come to you; but if I depart, I will send Him to you."* Here, Jesus says that it is better for Him to go away so that He can send His Spirit, whom He refers to as "the helper." It seems odd that Jesus starts by saying, *"... I tell you the truth ..."* Why would Jesus say this? Did He ever tell a lie? No. Everything that Jesus said was the truth. I believe Jesus started by saying "... I'm telling you the truth ..." because what He was about to say here in John 16:7 in regards to it being better for them that He goes away was going to be very difficult for them to understand. I believe that Jesus said this because He wanted to prepare them for what He was about to say.

Why was it better for us that Jesus went away? Well, the answer is simple. If Jesus was still here on earth today, you would need to travel to Israel to talk to Him, and you would have to stand in line with seven billion other people who would also want to talk to Him. Jesus was God in human form. He still needed to eat, sleep, and so on. So if Jesus did not go away and send His Spirit, you would not be able to have a relationship with Him because there would be billions of other people who would also want to spend time with Him. It would be nearly impossible for you to see Him. But when Jesus went away, He sent His Spirit down to earth, and the Holy Spirit (the Spirit of Christ) is now here. Today, He is our helper. He helps us in our weaknesses, He helps us to pray, He gives us the power to share the Gospel, and He reminds us of every word Jesus has spoken. Yes, it is so much better for you and me that Jesus went to heaven because now, through the Holy Spirit, we can have fellowship with Christ without needing to travel to Israel. We don't have to stand in line with billions of other people who also desire to have fellowship with Him. You can have fellowship with Jesus wherever you are right now.

When Jesus died on the cross, was buried and arose, He went to His disciples and commanded them not to leave Jerusalem, until the promise of His Father had been fulfilled. We can see this in Acts 1:4 (NIV), which states, *"On one occasion, while he was eating with them, he gave them this command: 'Do not leave Jerusalem, but wait for the gift my Father promised, which you have heard me speak about.'"* The promise Jesus was referring to was the Holy Spirit, and in Acts 1:8, Jesus continues, *"But you will receive power when the Holy Spirit comes on you; and you will be my witnesses in Jerusalem, and in all Judea and Samaria, and to the ends of the earth."* We see the promise fulfilled when the Holy Spirit was sent to earth on the day of Pentecost, ten days after Jesus ascended into heaven. Acts 2:1-4 (NKJV) states:

When the Day of Pentecost had fully come, they were all with one accord in one place. And suddenly there came a sound from heaven, as of a rushing mighty wind, and it filled the whole house where they were sitting. Then there appeared to them divided tongues, as of fire, and one sat upon each of them. And they were all filled with the Holy Spirit and began to speak with other tongues, as the Spirit gave them utterance.

Here, we see come together what Jesus and the Father promised. The day of Pentecost is the first time throughout the Bible that we see people get baptized with the Holy Spirit. The promise of the Holy Spirit is also for you and me today. God is the same today, Jesus is the same today, and the Holy Spirit is the same today, which means that you and I can experience this amazing life with the Holy Spirit. Yes, we can receive the Holy Spirit like the early disciples did in the Book of Acts.

On the day of Pentecost, Peter said in Acts 2:38 (NKJV), "... *Repent, and let every one of you be baptized in the name of Jesus Christ for the remission of sins; and you shall receive the gift of the Holy Spirit.*" Peter continued in verse 39, "*For the promise is to you and to your children, and to all who are afar off, as many as the Lord our God will call.*" The "promise" that Peter is referring to here is the gift of the Holy Spirit. This same promise was prophesied six hundred years before Jesus Christ spoke about it and before the early disciples received the Holy Spirit on the day of Pentecost. We read this in Ezekiel 36:26: "*I will give you a new heart and put a new spirit within you; I will take the heart of stone out of your flesh and give you a heart of flesh.*"

FOR THE

PROMISE

IS FOR YOU
AND YOUR CHILDREN
AND FOR ALL WHO ARE FAR OFF
FOR ALL WHOM THE LORD OUR GOD WILL CALL.

HOLY SPIRIT

Yes, 600 years before Peter and the other early disciples were filled with the Holy Spirit, it was prophesied that God would take out our heart of stone and give us a heart of flesh and a new spirit. This was prophesied not only by Ezekiel, but also by the prophet Joel. We read about what Joel prophesied from Peter in Acts 2:16-17: "*But this is what was spoken by the prophet Joel: 'And it shall come to pass in the last days, says God, that I will pour out of My Spirit on all flesh; your sons and your daughters shall prophesy, your young men shall see visions, your old men shall dream dreams.'"*

The promise of the Holy Spirit is also for you and me today. It was not only for those living in the time of the New Testament. Peter said, *"For the promise is to you and to your children ..."*

I have experienced the Holy Spirit spoken about by Jesus and prophesied about by Ezekiel 600 years before Christ. I have experienced the new spirit and new heart that Peter and the apostles spoke about on the day of Pentecost. And you can, too. Have you experienced it?

I would now like to look at how people throughout the Book of Acts received the Holy Spirit. We see this happen in Acts 8, where Philip traveled to Samaria. Here, we read how Philip preached the Gospel, healed the sick, cast out demons, and baptized people in water. Yes, many amazing things happened when Philip went to Samaria. While Philip was visiting Samaria, he realized that the people there who had repented and been baptized in water did not yet receive the Holy Spirit. When the apostles heard about this, Peter and John traveled to Samaria to pray for the believers to receive the Holy Spirit. We see this in Acts 8:15 (NIV), which states, *"When they arrived, they prayed for the new believers there that they might receive the Holy Spirit, because the Holy Spirit had not yet come on any of them; they had simply been baptized in the name of the Lord Jesus."* From Acts 8, we can see many different things. First, we see that people do not automatically receive the Holy

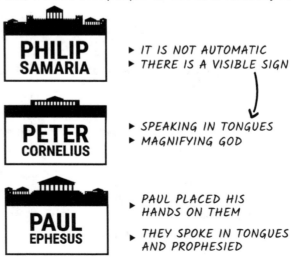

PHILIP
SAMARIA
- IT IS NOT AUTOMATIC
- THERE IS A VISIBLE SIGN

PETER
CORNELIUS
- SPEAKING IN TONGUES
- MAGNIFYING GOD

PAUL
EPHESUS
- PAUL PLACED HIS HANDS ON THEM
- THEY SPOKE IN TONGUES AND PROPHESIED

Spirit when they start believing in Jesus. We see how people, even after repenting and being baptized in water, still did not receive the Holy Spirit. And today, there are many believers all around the world who have faith in God, who have repented and got baptized in water, but they have not received the Holy Spirit. So we need someone to, like Philip and the other apostles, lay hands on and pray for those who have not received the Holy Spirit.

The second thing we learn from Acts 8 is that there is a sign when people receive the Holy Spirit, and the apostles questioned whether the people in Samaria had the Spirit because they did not have this sign. When the apostles laid hands on them and prayed for them to be filled with the Holy Spirit, everyone around them could recognize the moment they received the Spirit. But how could the apostles see that they did not have the Holy Spirit? And how could the other people see that they received the Spirit when the apostles prayed for them? Well, it is difficult to answer these questions if we only look at Acts 8. Therefore, we must look at other places in Acts to see a clear picture of what this "sign" is.

In Acts 10, we can see what the sign of the Holy Spirit is by reading about how Peter went to the house of Cornelius. Here, while Peter was speaking to Cornelius and his household, suddenly, they all received the Holy Spirit. But how did Peter know that? Well, because Acts 10:46 states, *"For they heard them speaking in tongues and praising God ..."* So speaking in tongues and praising God were the signs witnessed by Peter, which showed him that they had just received the Holy Spirit. We see another place where people received the Holy Spirit, accompanied by signs in Acts 19. In Acts 19, we read about how Paul was visiting some believers in Ephesus and how he preached the Gospel to them, baptized them in water and with the Holy Spirit. And in Acts 19:6, we read, *"And when Paul had laid hands on them, the Holy Spirit came upon them, and they spoke with tongues and prophesied."* Here, the sign of receiving the Holy Spirit was speaking in tongues and prophesying.

In Acts 8, 10, and 19, we can see that when people in the early church repented, got baptized in water, and received the Holy Spirit, something happened to show others that the Holy Spirit had been given to them. Yes, the signs were speaking in tongues and prophesying, or speaking in tongues and praising God. And today, it should be the same because this promise is also for us. Over the last years, I have prayed for hundreds of people who have received the Holy Spirit and started to speak in tongues. It is so amazing to see the Spirit of Jesus fill them and to witness them speaking in new tongues, just like we read about in the Bible. The promise of the Holy Spirit is not just something promised for those living two thousand years ago, but it is still a promise to us today. Yes, the Holy Spirit is for you and me.

Sometimes, throughout the Book of Acts, we read how people received the Holy Spirit immediately after being baptized in water. Other times, like in Acts 10, we read how people received the Holy Spirit first and then later got baptized in water. And other times, we read how people repented and got baptized in water but did not receive the Holy Spirit until someone prayed for them. Despite seeing a slightly different order in the Book of Acts, what is important to know is that you must experience this. As I have said before, it is not enough for you to read about it, hear about it, or dream about it. No, you need to experience it. The Holy Spirit is for you, and speaking in tongues is also for you.

I would now like to take the time to discuss speaking in tongues because there is a lot of misunderstanding about this topic. Many people do not understand that there are different kinds of tongues, and I would like to address this. To speak in tongues is to speak a language. The word "tongues" actually means "language." And when I speak to people, I speak in tongues because I speak to them in a language. This is referred to as a "physical language," and this is something we all have. From the moment I was born, I was surrounded by a physical language, and as I grew up, I also learned to speak that language. I learned to speak Danish, and later on, I learned a little bit of German and English.

There is also a spiritual language, and I believe that this is for everyone who is born by the Spirit. I refer to this language as "personal tongues" or a "personal prayer language." And this is what Paul is referring to in 1 Corinthians 14:2 (NKJV), which states, *"For he who speaks in a tongue does not speak to men but to God, for no one understands him; however, in the spirit he speaks mysteries."* Paul again speaks about this "personal tongue" in 1 Corinthians 14:4: *"He who speaks in a tongue edifies himself ..."* In these two verses, Paul is speaking about a "personal tongue," which you do not use to talk to people around you, but which you use to speak mysteries to God. Though no one around you understands what you are saying, as Paul says, you are edifying yourself by speaking in this language. In 1 Corinthians 14:14 (NIV), Paul states, *"For if I pray in a tongue, my spirit prays, but my mind is unfruitful."* And he later continues to say in 1 Corinthians 14:18, "*I thank God that I speak in tongues more than all of you.*" I believe that here in 1 Corinthians 14:14 and 1 Corinthians 14:18, Paul is speaking about the "personal tongues" or "personal prayer language." It is the language that we use to speak mysteries to God, to edify ourselves, and where, though our mind is unfruitful, our spirit is fruitful. I believe that this "personal tongue" is for everyone, and I have seen thousands of people all around the world receive this tongue.

Aside from the physical language and the "personal tongue," there are two other types of tongues. One of these tongues is used for edifying the church, and the other is used for reaching out to the world. I have witnessed the tongue meant to edify the church many times. One time, I was at a Kickstart in Norway. During the meeting, people were praying as my wife sang a song. Suddenly, God came with His Holy Spirit, and a man stood up and spoke very loudly in tongues. He started to speak very loudly, and though no one could understand what he was saying with their physical ears, we could sense in our spirits that it was a different kind of tongue. Yes, we knew that it was not the "personal tongue," but that it was a tongue meant to edify the church. Suddenly, a woman stood up and translated what he said into a physical tongue so that people could understand what he was saying. And as he continued with the tongue, she continued with the interpretation. That tongue edified everyone at the Kickstart, and it was incredible. I have seen this many times all over the world. I have also received an interpretation for a tongue before. I could not understand what the tongue was saying with my physical ears, but words came to me in my spirit, and I interpreted the tongue for the church, and everyone was edified. This is the tongue Paul is referring to in 1 Corinthians 14:27-28 (NIV): "*If anyone speaks in a tongue, two—or at the most three—should speak, one at a time, and someone must interpret. If there is no interpreter, the speaker should keep quiet in the church and speak to himself and to God.*" So here, we read about the tongue that is meant to build up or strengthen the body and that when we come together as a body, God uses this to speak to us. But here, we also read how someone needs to come with the interpretation so that the church can be edified.

Lastly, the fourth kind of tongue, meant to reach out to the world, does not need an interpretation. Yes, people can understand this tongue. We can see this kind of tongue in Acts 2:6 (NIV), which states, "*When they heard this sound, a crowd came together in bewilderment, because each one heard their own language being spoken."* Here, we read how the apostles spoke in tongues and how people were shocked to hear them speaking in their language. Yes, people who spoke different languages understood what the apostles were saying. And this is something we can also experience today.

I would now like to share a testimony with you. A few years ago, I was in Germany, and as I was walking, a man approached me and started talking to me. I could immediately see that he was a Satanist from the satanic symbols on his body and a "666" tattoo on his knuckles. As I started to talk to him, I suddenly felt something I had never felt before. I felt like I should speak to him in tongues. This was odd for me because I don't ever speak to people in tongues because I know that it is a language between God and me, and other people would not understand me. But at that moment, I felt like that was what I needed to do, so I put my hand on him, looked into his eyes, and started to speak in tongues. I could feel that my "personal tongue" changed. It sounded different from how I normally speak in tongues. I still did not understand what I was saying, but I continued to pray in tongues to him. And when I stopped, he stepped back with eyes wide and said, "How did you know?" Confused, I asked him, "How did I know what?" Again, he said, "How did you know?" But I did not know what he was talking about. Then he asked, "How did you learn our language?" He then started to tell me about how he and his brother, as young kids, developed a secret language that only they could understand and that, when I spoke to him in tongues, I spoke to him about God in that language. When I left him, I turned and looked back at him and saw him standing with his arms raised worshiping God. When I look back on that event, I can see how, at that moment, the Holy Spirit came over me, and I received the tongue that we read about in Acts 2. It was so powerful.

I believe that the kind of tongue we read about in Acts 2 has gotten lost in the church, and we no longer see many people experience this. In the early church, everyone knew that there were different kinds of tongues, and it was natural for them to experience them. They understood that there was a physical tongue, a "personal tongue," a tongue for edifying the church, and a tongue for reaching out to the world. Just like you receive a physical tongue in the physical world, when you are born in the Spirit, you receive a spiritual tongue, and I truly believe that this spiritual tongue ("personal tongue") is for everyone who is born again. This tongue is amazing! We can use it whenever we want to communicate with God, and it edifies us. And when we have received it, it is important that we use it. The other two kinds of tongues (the one used to edify the church and the one used to reach out to the world) are not tongues that we can use whenever we want to. I cannot just decide to speak to people in another language. No, this is something that God does through you when He decides to. So, unlike the physical tongue and "personal tongue," we cannot use the other two tongues at will. If you have experienced the tongue used to edify the church and the tongue used to reach out to the world, then you probably understand what I am talking about. But if you never heard what I have shared in this lesson, though it may sound complicated, it is very simple.

I would now like to focus on the "personal tongue." This "personal tongue," or "personal prayer language," is for everyone who has received the Holy Spirit. I absolutely love witnessing people receive the Holy Spirit and start speaking in tongues. And as I have previously said, I have witnessed this all over the world with thousands of people. Receiving the Holy Spirit and speaking in this "personal tongue" is very simple, especially when you do not have a religious background. Yes, I have seen thousands of people without any religious background repent, receive the Holy Spirit, and start speaking in tongues. But sometimes, we meet people who have a difficult time speaking in tongues because of what they grew up hearing in church. Some people have heard that speaking in tongues is not for everyone or that it is demonic. Often, when people hear these things, they develop a fear of tongues.

Some years ago, I visited Cape Town, South Africa. There, I met a man who really wanted the Holy Spirit, but throughout his life, he heard many wrong teachings about speaking in tongues, including how tongues are not for everyone. Together, we sat down and talked, and I started to explain things about the Holy Spirit and speaking in tongues. While I was talking, he suddenly stood up and said, "I have it now! I understand it now! Lay your hands on me!" And the second I put my hands on him to pray for him to receive the Holy Spirit, he shouted out in new tongues. What happened while I was talking to him? Well, the answer is that he got a revelation. Yes, he suddenly understood how speaking in tongues worked, and he saw that he had believed false theology regarding the Holy Spirit and speaking in tongues. When he recognized those false doctrines, he received the Holy Spirit and spoke in tongues instantly.

It is important to understand that we must receive tongues in faith. Yes, we need to believe God's Word and then receive His promise for us. You can receive the Holy Spirit in different ways. One way is to pray to God and ask Him for His Spirit. Jesus actually talks about this in Matthew 7:7-8 (NIV): *"Ask and it will be given to you; seek and you will find; knock and the door will be opened to you. For everyone who asks receives; the one who seeks finds; and to the one who knocks, the door will be opened."* In this verse, Jesus is referring to how to receive the Holy Spirit. And in Luke 11:13 (NIV), Jesus says, *"If you then, though you are evil, know how to give good gifts to your children, how much more will your Father in heaven give the Holy Spirit to those who ask him!"* This verse is also referring to how much God wants to give you His Spirit. So, we can see that when we want God's Spirit, we must ask, seek, knock, pray, and He will give you the Holy Spirit. Another way to receive the Holy Spirit is by having other people with the Spirit place their hands on you and pray for you to receive Him. We see an example of this in Acts 8, where the apostles laid their hands on the people and they received the Holy Spirit. We also read in Acts 19:6, how Paul came and laid hands on the people, and they also received the Holy Spirit.

I have met people who have the Holy Spirit but do not speak in tongues because they have misunderstood it. They often think that God will open their mouth and that their mouth will suddenly start to speak by itself. No, this is not how it works. God will not possess your mouth and make you speak. You need to open your mouth yourselves and start to speak.

When I want to speak in tongues, I need to open my mouth and speak, and then it will continue to flow out of me. I don't wait for God to take over my mouth and make me speak in tongues. No, I start on my own. When we baptize people in water, we lay our hands on them and pray for the Holy Spirit to come over them. Sometimes, when the Holy Spirit comes over someone, they immediately start to speak in tongues. At other times, we tell them, "Open your mouth and speak. Just let it out." When they do this and say the first few words, it suddenly flows out of them like living water.

It is important to understand that everyone is different. Some people get baptized, and immediately after they are baptized, they stand up from the water and burst out in new tongues. When I received the Holy Spirit many years ago, I did not feel much. But when the person praying for me to receive the Holy Spirit told me to open my mouth and speak, I just started. In the beginning, I just spoke out a few simple words, and then, suddenly, it naturally flowed out from me.

How do we know that we are speaking in tongues and not just saying our own words? John 7:37-38 (NKJV) can help us determine whether we are speaking in tongues, where Jesus states, "... *If anyone thirsts, let him come to Me and drink. He who believes in Me, as the Scripture has said, out of his heart will flow rivers of living water.*" When people receive the Holy Spirit and start to speak in tongues, words flow out of their heart like living water, and we can continue speaking in tongues for hours because we do not need to concentrate on what we are saying, as it is not the mind that is fruitful but the spirit. When we speak in tongues, we are connecting to God, and our spirit is being edified.

Depending on your age, you may remember the old modem that people used to connect to the Internet many years ago. My family and I had a modem that we called the "Internet," and the modem would make numerous beeping sounds as it tried to connect. And when that modem finally connected to the Internet, we could access a lot of information on our computer. Similar to the modem that needs to connect to the Internet to get information, when I speak in tongues, I connect to God, and I can hear God speak to me. So I want to encourage you and tell you that if you can speak in tongues, then do it. If you do not have it, then receive it and start to use it to edify yourself and connect to God.

So what do we believe? Let's go back to the beginning. When Jesus was here on earth, He taught about the Holy Spirit and said in John 16:7 that it was better for Him to go away so that He could send down His Helper, the Holy Spirit. He taught that the Holy Spirit would help us, comfort us, convict us, teach us truth, and remind us of every word that Jesus said. Then, Jesus died on the cross, was buried, and arose. Before he ascended into heaven, He commanded His disciples to stay in Jerusalem until the Holy Spirit was sent down to earth (Acts 1:4). Then, Jesus ascended to heaven to sit beside God's right hand and sent down His Holy Spirit on the day of Pentecost. We can read, in Acts 2, how the apostles were filled with the Holy Spirit and began to speak in tongues. We see people receive the Holy Spirit and speak in tongues in Acts 8, where Philip met the eunuch in Samaria. In Acts 10, we see where Peter traveled to the house of Cornelius. And in Acts 19, Paul traveled to the believers in Ephesus. When people receive the Holy Spirit today, they should also speak in tongues and prophesy or speak in tongues and praise God, as people did in the Bible. The Holy Spirit is for everyone. If you do not have the Holy Spirit, pray and ask God to give you His Spirit, or ask people who have the Holy Spirit to pray for you to receive the Spirit of God. And when you receive the Holy Spirit, you need to speak out in faith. You need to say the first few words and then the rest will flow out of you like rivers of living water. When you speak in the "personal tongue," you edify yourself and connect to God. I believe that if you have the Holy Spirit, then you have tongues. I am not saying that those who don't speak in tongues do not have the Holy Spirit because there are people who have received the Holy Spirit, but just don't know how to speak in tongues, possibly because of wrong teachings in the church. So if you are sure that you have the Holy Spirit, then you already have tongues inside of you. You just need to open your mouth and let it out.

QUESTIONS & ANSWERS

DO I NEED TO SPEAK IN TONGUES TO BE SAVED?

No, you do not need to speak in tongues to be saved, but you need the Holy Spirit to be born again. As we have seen in the Bible, speaking in tongues is a sign that people have received the Holy Spirit. Throughout the years, we have met people whom we truly believed had received the Holy Spirit, but they had not spoken in tongues because they had believed in false doctrines. Some of them had even grown up hearing that speaking in tongues is not from God. I believe that if someone receives the Holy Spirit but does not speak in tongues, they are still born again.

When I attended church on the evening of April 5, 1995, I did not know anything about speaking in tongues. Other than the Danish Lutheran church, that evening was one of my first times attending a church. The pastor asked everyone who did not have the Holy Spirit to come to the front so that he could pray for them to receive God's Spirit. I still remember how my heart started to beat fast, and I just knew that I needed to go up and get prayed for. I went up to the front, and the pastor laid his hands on me and began to pray. And when he did this, something incredible happened. I experienced something like a light come into my body, and I received the Holy Spirit. At the time, I did not know anything about speaking in tongues. So even though I received the Holy Spirit on the evening of April 5, 1995, it still took me a few months before I started to speak in tongues.

A few months later, some people came to me and said, "Torben, we are going to pray for you. If you believe you have the Holy Spirit, just open your mouth and speak in tongues." When these people prayed for me, I opened my mouth in faith and spoke in tongues. I believe that at that moment when I first spoke in tongues, I let out what I had already received on the evening of April 5, 1995.

So speaking in tongues is a sign of Holy Spirit, but some people have received the Holy Spirit and do not have this sign. We cannot be sure if someone has the Holy Spirit without seeing the sign. It is important, when you pray for people to receive the Holy Spirit and speak in tongues, that you encourage them to open their mouth and speak in faith because we want to be sure that people are fully born again and have received the Holy Spirit.

DO I NEED THE HOLY SPIRIT TO BE SAVED?

Yes, you do need the Holy Spirit to be born again and saved. It is important to understand that the Holy Spirit plays a crucial part in your coming to and living for God. He plays an active part in leading someone to repentance, He works through baptism in water by setting people free and washing away their sins, and He leads and helps people in their walk with God.

You need the Holy Spirit to be born again and to be made into a new creation. Sadly, there are many people who come to faith and repent and stop there, thinking that it is enough. Many people think, "Oh, God has changed me, and I am now saved!" But the truth is, if you only come to faith, and repent, you are not fully born again. It took me six years to reach the point where I repented, got baptized in water, and received the Holy Spirit. It took me six years before I got born again. Sometimes, it takes people a long time to be born again, and for others, it takes a short time. To be born again, you must repent, get baptized in water, and receive the Holy Spirit. Don't stop before you are born again. You need to be set free from your sin through baptism in water and you need to receive the Holy Spirit to lead you and help you grow in Christ.

I believe that the Holy Spirit will draw everyone who sincerely wants to follow Jesus to the whole truth and that everyone who wants to follow Jesus will come across this teaching that I am sharing in this book by reading the Word of God, or by reading this book. And I believe that everyone who is led to this teaching will be transformed through the understanding of needing to be born again. If you are reading this book, and you are not born again, I encourage you to keep praying and seeking God until you have received everything God wants to give you.

HOW TO BAPTIZE SOMEONE WITH THE HOLY SPIRIT?

As I have said in this lesson, I have prayed for hundreds who have received the Holy Spirit. In the beginning, when I started to pray for people to receive the Holy Spirit, only one out of 20 people I prayed for actually received the Holy Spirit and started to speak in tongues. As I grew with God, I started to see about five out of twenty people that I prayed for receive the Holy Spirit and speak in tongues. As I continued to work with people, I learned more about how to help people to correct their misunderstandings and false doctrines regarding the Holy Spirit and then about ten out of twenty people I prayed for received the Holy Spirit and spoke in tongues. As I learned more about how to share the Gospel, and how to help people understand repentance, baptism in water, and with the Holy Spirit, I started to see about eighteen out of twenty people I prayed for receive the Holy Spirit and speak in tongues. And then when we had longer time to work with people and help them correct any misunderstandings, I saw one hundred percent of the people I prayed for receive the Holy Spirit and speak in tongues. Why did I see it increase as I grew with God? Well, because the Holy Spirit and tongues is a promise from God, and it is for everyone. But we have to understand that everyone is different, and we all have a unique story. Sometimes the things we have learned can prevent us from receiving the Holy Spirit and speaking in tongues.

When someone wants to receive the Holy Spirit and speak in tongues but seems unable to, it is sometimes wrong doctrines that hinder them from receiving. They may be waiting for emotions to come and overwhelm them and for their mouth to suddenly start speaking on its own. But this isn't how it works. Other times, people may want to receive the Holy Spirit and speak in tongues but do not because they are still living in sin and have not really repented and turned to Christ. Therefore, they cannot receive the Holy Spirit. Other people, as I have previously said, have already received the Holy Spirit but did not open their mouth and start to speak in tongues because no one told them about it, and they weren't sure how it worked. So each person is different.

It is often easier for people to receive the Holy Spirit and speak in tongues if they have no church background. Why is this? Well, it is because they have not accepted the traditions of man and wrong doctrines that many people have grown up hearing in church. As I have previously said, there are wrong teachings that say that tongues are not for today, and some even teach that it is demonic.

When you find someone who has repented and is baptized in water, lay hands on them and pray for them to receive the Holy Spirit. Take the time to pray for them and speak in tongues while you are praying for them. Sometimes you may notice, by their facial expression, that the Holy Spirit is filling them up and sometimes you will see their mouth start to open. Just encourage them to speak the first words. And when they just start with those first few words, it will just naturally flow out of them. So don't be afraid to learn to pray for people to receive the Spirit of God. We are not only called to lead people to Christ and baptize people in water, but we are also called to lay hands on people and baptize them with the Holy Spirit. As Jesus said in Matthew 10:8 (NKJV), *"... Freely you have received, freely give."* So I encourage you to be bold. Pray for people and see how God will work through you. Remember that you are a disciple/apprentice, and as you learn, it will become easier and easier.

WHO IS THE HOLY SPIRIT?

The Holy Spirit does many amazing things in our lives. I know that I have focused on speaking in tongues a lot in this lesson, but He also does so much more than allow you to speak in tongues. I decided to focus on speaking in tongues in this lesson because it is a clear sign that someone has received the Holy Spirit, and it is very important for people to have Him.

I would now like to go through the tasks of the Holy Spirit. First off, it is important to understand that the Holy Spirit is the Spirit of Christ on earth. When Jesus went to heaven and sent down His Holy Spirit, we become His body when we receive the Holy Spirit, so that, in Him, we can live the life that Christ has called us to. The Holy Spirit does many different things. Firstly, the Bible says that He is our helper and that He reminds us of what Jesus said. We can see this in John 14:26 (NKJV), which states, *"But the Helper, the Holy Spirit, whom the Father will send in My name, He will teach you all things, and bring to your remembrance all things that I said to you."* So, the Holy Spirit is our Teacher.

Another task of the Holy Spirit is to convict the world of sin, righteousness, and judgment. We can see this in John 16:7-8, which states, *"Nevertheless I tell you the truth. It is to your advantage that I go away; for if I do not go away, the Helper will not come to you; but if I depart, I will send Him to you. And when He has come, He will convict the world of sin, and of righteousness, and of judgment..."* The Holy Spirit is the one who reveals sin in peoples' lives and works in their lives to produce righteousness. The Holy Spirit is also the Spirit of truth. We can see this in John 16:13-15 (NKJV), as it states:

However, when He, the Spirit of truth, has come, He will guide you into all truth; for

He will not speak on His own authority, but whatever He hears He will speak; and He will tell you things to come. He will glorify Me, for He will take of what is Mine and declare it to you. All things that the Father has are Mine. Therefore I said that He will take of Mine and declare it to you.

He is the Spirit that came to speak the truth. And we know that the truth is so important, as John 8:32 (NKJV) states, "And you shall know the truth, and the truth shall make you free."

Ephesians 1:17-18 (NKJV) states:

...That the God of our Lord Jesus Christ, the Father of glory, may give to you the spirit of wisdom and revelation in the knowledge of Him, the eyes of your understanding being enlightened; that you may know what is the hope of His calling, what are the riches of the glory of His inheritance in the saints...

From these verses, we can see that the Holy Spirit is also the Spirit of wisdom and revelation and that He helps us to discern the will of God better and better.

Paul states in 1 Corinthians 11:1 (NKJV): *"Imitate me, just as I also imitate Christ."* It is very interesting that Paul said this because he did not walk with Jesus on earth like John, James, Peter, and the other disciples did. He never saw Jesus with his own eyes like the early disciples did, but he still said that people should imitate him as he imitates Christ. It almost seems as though Paul knew Jesus better than the other disciples who actually walked on earth with Jesus for over three years. But how is it possible that Paul could know Jesus better than John, James, Peter, and the others? This is possible by the Spirit who reminds us of Jesus' words, of truth, of revelation, and of wisdom. It is possible for us to know Jesus as the early disciples did because we have free access to a relationship with Jesus Christ through the Spirit of God. Spending time with the Holy Spirit was so important to Paul, and we can see this in 1 Corinthians 14:18, which states, "I thank my God I speak with tongues more than you all..." I believe it is so important to spend time with the Holy Spirit, to speak in tongues, to let the Holy Spirit teach you as you read the Word of God, and to allow the Holy Spirit to guide you and give you wisdom and understanding.

The Holy Spirit also gives gifts to the body of Christ. We can read about this in 1 Corinthians 12:7-11 (NKJV), which states:

But the manifestation of the Spirit is given to each one for the profit of all: for to one is given the word of wisdom through the Spirit, to another the word of knowledge through the same Spirit, to another faith by the same Spirit, to another gifts of healings by the same Spirit, to another the working of miracles, to another prophecy, to another discerning of spirits, to another different kinds of tongues, to another the interpretation of tongues. But one and the same Spirit works all these things, distributing to each one individually as He wills.

So He empowers us with supernatural gifts. The Holy Spirit is also the seed of our salvation, and we can read this in Ephesians 1:13-15 (NIV), which states:

And you also were included in Christ when you heard the message of truth, the gospel of your salvation. When you believed, you were marked in him with a seal, the promised Holy Spirit, who is a deposit guaranteeing our inheritance until the redemption of those who are God's possession—to the praise of his glory.

It is not good for man to be alone. God, in Genesis 2:18 (NIV) states, "*... It is not good for the man to be alone. I will make a helper suitable for him.*" Although He was referring to how He was going to create a wife for Adam, it is clear that it is not good for us to be alone. So that is why the Holy Spirit was sent down to help us. The Holy Spirit also helps us by interceding for us when we pray. We read about this in Romans 8:26-27 (NIV), which says:

In the same way, the Spirit helps us in our weakness. We do not know what we ought to pray for, but the Spirit himself intercedes for us through wordless groans. And he who searches our hearts knows the mind of the Spirit, because the Spirit intercedes for God's people in accordance with the will of God.

Sometimes when I pray, I don't know how to pray in my own words. When this happens, I just pray in tongues and then experience the Holy Spirit come and help me to pray in my own language. He gives me the words and helps me to pray.

The Holy Spirit, living inside born again believers, also makes believers new and gives them eternal life. This is clear in Romans 8:10-11 (NIV), which says:

But if Christ is in you, then even though your body is subject to death because of sin, the Spirit gives life because of righteousness. And if the Spirit of him who raised Jesus from the dead is living in you, he who raised Christ from the dead will also give life to your mortal bodies because of his Spirit who lives in you.

Like Jesus was raised from the dead, the Holy Spirit raises us from the dead, gives eternal life to our dead body, transforms us, and helps us to be holy.

The Holy Spirit also produces good fruit in us. In Galatians 5:22-23 (NKJV), we read about the fruits of the Holy Spirit, as it states, *"But the fruit of the Spirit is love, joy, peace, longsuffering, kindness, goodness, faithfulness, gentleness, self-control ..."* The fruit of the Spirit is the long-term evidence that someone has the Holy Spirit. If those fruits do not develop in a person's life over time, then it is likely they do not have the Spirit of God living in them. Neither does the Holy Spirit bring a lot of focus on Himself, as He is there to bring focus on Jesus Christ and His words. It is all about Jesus, so we should not worship or pray to the Holy Spirit. Rather, the Spirit helps us to worship and focus on Christ and pray to our Father in heaven. So the Holy Spirit does much more than enabling someone to speak in tongues. Tongues is an important part of being filled with the Spirit and prayer to God.

88

THE GOOD NEWS

LESSON FOUR

Welcome to **Lesson Four** of this **Kickstart Package**. Six thousand three hundred people die every hour. One hundred fifty thousand people die every day. That is a total of 55.3 million people who die every year. One day, it will be your turn to die. We don't know when or how we are going to die, but we know that the day will come. Around 1.2 million people die in motor vehicle accidents every year, and those people did not wake up in the morning expecting to die that day. Life is short, and whether you are here on earth for 20 years or 100 years, you will eventually die. But there is good news. John 3:16 states, *"For God so loved the world that he gave his one and only Son, that whoever believes in him shall not perish but have eternal life."* And 1 John 5:10-12 states:

Whoever believes in the Son of God accepts this testimony. Whoever does not believe God has made him out to be a liar, because they have not believed the testimony God has given about his Son. And this is the testimony: God has given us eternal life, and this life is in his Son. Whoever has the Son has life; whoever does not have the Son of God does not have life.

As we can see in these verses, we can have eternal life through the Son of God, Jesus Christ.

Welcome to **Lesson Four** of this **Kickstart Package**. In this lesson, I will use many Bible verses to share the Gospel from the beginning to the end. We will start in the book of Genesis, the first book of the Bible, and read about the Garden of Eden, how everything was perfect and how it all went wrong. We will end in Revelation, the last book of the Bible, where everything will once again be perfect, as God created it to be from the very beginning.

THE BEGINNING

In the book of Genesis, we read how God, in the very beginning, created heaven and earth in six days. After each day, we read something like, "... *And God saw that it was good. And there was evening, and there was morning—the third day*" (Genesis 1:12-13) and "*...And God saw that it was good. And there was evening, and there was morning—the fourth day*" (Genesis 1:18-19). At the end of Genesis 1, we read, in Genesis 1:31, "*God saw all that he had made, and it was very good. And there was evening, and there was morning—the sixth day.*" So we can see from these verses, that what God created, in the beginning, was a perfect, amazing, and beautiful world.

In Genesis 2, we read how God created man and put him in the garden with the Tree of Life and the Tree of Knowledge of Good and Evil. We can see this in Genesis 2:15-17, which states:

The Lord God took the man and put him in the Garden of Eden to work it and take care of it. And the Lord God commanded the man, "You are free to eat from any tree in the garden; but you must not eat from the tree of the knowledge of good and evil, for when you eat from it you will certainly die."

Adam and his wife, Eve, walked with God, and we read how they were both naked but not ashamed. They did not feel ashamed of their nakedness because they never sinned. And we can read how they walked with God and lived in a perfect world – a world without death, sickness, wars, murders, rape, earthquakes, tsunamis, fear, depression, suicide, and so on. Yes, it was a world that is so different from ours today. If you don't think our world is so bad, just look at the news. We hear about things like wars, sickness, death, and murder nearly every day.

THE FALL

But how did the perfect world that God created end up so evil? Well, the answer is sin. In Genesis 3, we read how Adam and Eve ate from the wrong tree, called the

Tree of Knowledge of Good and Evil. Yes, they ate from the tree that God told them not to eat from, and when they ate from that tree, their eyes were opened, sin entered them, and they suddenly recognized their nakedness. And we read how they tried to cover their nakedness with fig leaves and how they hid from God when, in Genesis 3:9, God searched for them and shouted out, *"... Where are you?"*

God desires to have fellowship with us and this is what we were created for. But because Adam and Eve ate from the Tree of Knowledge of Good and Evil, they became aware of sin and everything changed. Genesis 3:22-23 states:

And the Lord God said, "The man has now become like one of us, knowing good and evil. He must not be allowed to reach out his hand and take also from the tree of life and eat, and live forever." So the Lord God banished him from the Garden of Eden to work the ground from which he had been taken.

This verse can seem a little strange if this is the first time you are reading it. But God had to banish them from the garden because He no longer wanted man to live forever. It was so important that man was banished from the garden because if they ate from the Tree of Life after sin entered them and lived forever, man would have a never-ending problem with sin that would continually get worse for all eternity. So man was banished from the garden, and divided from God. And because Adam and Eve ate from the Tree of Knowledge of Good and Evil, sin came into the world and death entered every man because every man has sinned. We see this in Romans 5:12, which states, *"Therefore, just as sin entered the world through one man, and death through sin, and in this way death came to all people, because all sinned—."*

After Adam and Eve were banished from the garden of Eden, we read how they had children and how one of the sons, Caine, killed his brother, Abel. And this was the first murder. The world changed and it was no longer a good world without murder. It was no longer the perfect world God created in the beginning. And people started to live more in sin and grow further away from God. They did many things that were evil in the sight of God. And we read how it didn't take long before God regretted that He created man because of their evil deeds. We read this in Genesis 6:5-6, which states: *"The Lord saw how great the wickedness of the human race had become on the earth, and that every inclination of the thoughts of the human heart was only evil all the time. The Lord regretted that he had made human beings on the earth, and his heart was deeply troubled."*

We need to understand that God is not responsible for all the evil we see on the earth today. Like you and I, He doesn't like it either. In fact, He hates it even more than we do. I know many people say, "Oh, I cannot believe in a good God because of all of the evil on earth." But in response, I would say that all of the evil things we see on earth actually confirm that what we read in the Bible is correct. God hates our evil deeds so much that He even wanted to destroy all of mankind. But then, in Genesis 6, we read how He found Noah, a man who found favor in the eyes of the Lord. God told Noah to build an ark so that He could destroy the world and everyone in it and restart the human race with Noah and his family. But as soon as Noah and his family came out of the ark, once again, sin became a problem. Yes, Noah got drunk and people committed evil in the sight of the Lord. Why did it all go wrong again? Well, the answer is sin. Sin is not only in the world, but it is also inside of man. Yes, from the moment Adam and Eve ate from the Tree of Knowledge of Good and Evil, sin entered man and since then, sin has become part of our DNA. And it is inside everyone who is not born again.

SIN IS THE PROBLEM

Sin is the problem. Man sinned and the one who sinned shall die. So man has fallen and we cannot change ourselves. We need a way to start over and a way to get rid of our sinful nature that is embedded in our DNA. We need help, we need a savior. The good news is that we do have a savior and His name is Jesus. Jesus was Emmanuel, which means "God with us." He came to save us from our sins and I like to think of Him as the first born of the new race of people who will be born again and belong to Him. But before we talk about Jesus and what He did for us so that we can be born again, get a new nature, and eternal life, we need to look at sin. Jesus, in Matthew 5:21-22, states:

You have heard that it was said to the people long ago, "You shall not murder, and anyone who murders will be subject to judgment." But I tell you that anyone who is angry with a brother or sister will be subject to judgment. Again, anyone who says to a brother or sister, "Raca," is answerable to the court. And anyone who says, "You fool!" will be in danger of the fire of hell.

Wow, these are strong words. And He continues to talk about lust and adultery in Matthew 5:26-30, which states:

You have heard that it was said, "You shall not commit adultery." But I tell you that anyone who looks at a woman lustfully has already committed adultery with her in his heart. If your right eye causes you to stumble, gouge it out and throw it away. It is better for you to lose one part of your body than for your whole body to be thrown into hell. And if your right hand causes you to stumble, cut it off and throw it away. It is better for you to lose one part of your body than for your whole body to go into hell.

As we can see from these verses, if you look lustfully at someone, you have already committed adultery with that person in your heart. And if this is what Jesus says about anger and lust, what about lying or stealing? Have you ever stolen something? Have you ever lied? The question is not if you think you are a good person, the question is, are you good enough for heaven? Have you kept God's law perfectly? Are you without sin? James 2:10 says, *"For whoever keeps the whole law and yet stumbles at just one point is guilty of breaking all of it."* The truth is that we have all sinned. If we have only broken one of God's laws, we are guilty of breaking them all. We have all fallen, and we all have a sinful nature.

Imagine that I have a special camera that can film your whole life and that I made a five-minute video of your life for everyone in the world to watch. But this camera is special and it can see everything you do. Yes, it can see what you do in the dark when you think no one is watching you, and it can see inside of your heart and mind. It can see when you look at someone with lust, it knows every bad thought you have ever had, and it sees everything wrong you have ever done. But this special camera doesn't film everything because it doesn't film all of the good things you have done. It doesn't film all of the times you have given to the homeless, or all of the times you have donated to charity. No, it doesn't film any of this. You need to understand that the good things you have done are not pluses on your account and the bad things you have done are not minuses on your account. You will not die and stand before God, hoping that you have more pluses than minuses on your account. The good things you have done amount to zero because the good things you have done are what have been expected from you from the beginning. Therefore, the good things can never justify the wrong things you have done.

So imagine I put together this five minute video of your life of all of the wrong things you have done, including every sexual thought you have ever had, every time you have broken God's law, every evil deed you have ever done, and so on. Now imagine I show that video to everyone. How would you feel if your family, friends, and the entire world saw every bad thing you have ever done and thought? Do you think they would still think you are a good person? The truth is, if this video of your life was shown to the whole world, you would feel so ashamed for people to see the evil inside of you. And so would I. I would be so ashamed that I would run and hide from everyone. But if you would feel ashamed if people saw these bad things you have done and thought, knowing that they are also just as guilty as you, imagine how ashamed you would feel standing before a holy and righteous God.

People often compare themselves to others around them. For example, you may look at your neighbor and say, "I am better than he is. I never went to jail, and I never did drugs like him." But a very dangerous sin is self-righteousness – thinking you are good enough. The truth is we are not good enough. We have all broken God's law. And we see this in Ecclesiastes 7:20, which states, "Indeed, there is no one on earth who is righteous, no one who does what is right and never sins" and Romans 3:23, which says, "... for all have sinned and fall short of the glory of God...". God could send every one of us to hell, and He would still be good, loving, and righteous because He is not the problem – we are. But instead, God did something absolutely incredible. He gave us a chance to experience forgiveness and a new life through His son, Jesus. No one can become righteous by their own deeds through keeping the law. And we can see this in Romans 3:20, which states, "Therefore no one will be declared righteous in God's sight by the works of the law; rather, through the law we become conscious of our sin" and Romans 3:22, which says, "This righteousness is given through faith in Jesus Christ to all who believe. There is no difference between

Jew and Gentile..." So seeing the fallen state of man and knowing that we could never become righteous through the law, God sent His son Jesus to die for us.

JESUS IS THE ANSWER

Jesus is the answer to our problem. He is the lamb of God who came to take away the sins of the world. Matthew 1:21 states, *"She will give birth to a son, and you are to give him the name Jesus, because he will save his people from their sins."* So God loved the world so much that He sent His only son, Jesus, to save us from our sins. Jesus was born of a virgin and, as stated in John 1:9, He is the true light that gives light to everyone. Jesus walked here on earth and He never sinned. He was the only man without sin. When He was about 30 years old, He was baptized in water and the Holy Spirit came over Him, which we read about in Matthew 3:16-17, which states, *"As soon as Jesus was baptized, he went up out of the water. At that moment heaven was opened, and he saw the Spirit of God descending like a dove and alighting on him. And a voice from heaven said, 'This is my Son, whom I love; with him I am well pleased.'"* After Jesus was baptized, He went out into the desert for forty days and forty nights, where He was tempted by Satan. When Jesus came out of the desert, He started to heal the sick and preach the Gospel of the Kingdom of God. And from that time on, Jesus preached, as stated in Matthew 4:17, *"Repent, for the kingdom of heaven has come near."* We can see what Jesus did in Matthew 4:23, which states, *"Jesus went throughout Galilee, teaching in their synagogues, proclaiming the good news of the kingdom, and healing every disease and sickness among the people."* He also said that we must be born again. We read this in John 3:5-7, which states, *"Jesus answered, 'Very truly I tell you, no one can enter the kingdom of God unless they are born of water and the Spirit. Flesh gives birth to flesh, but the Spirit gives birth to spirit. You should not be surprised at my saying, 'You must be born again.'"*

So Jesus walked on earth, preached the Gospel, healed the sick, called people to follow Him as His disciples, and said that we must be born again. Throughout Matthew, we can read some of the things He said to people who wanted to follow Him. Matthew 16:24-25 states, *"Then Jesus said to his disciples, 'Whoever wants to be my disciple must deny themselves and take up their cross and follow me. For whoever wants to save their life will lose it, but whoever loses their life for me will find it.' "* And Matthew 10:34-39 states:

Do not suppose that I have come to bring peace to the earth. I did not come to bring peace, but a sword. For I have come to turn "a man against his father, a daughter against her mother, a daughter-in-law against her mother-in-law—a man's enemies will be the members of his own household." Anyone who loves their father or mother more than me is not worthy of me; anyone who loves their son or daughter more than me is not worthy of me. Whoever does not take up their cross and follow me is not worthy of me. Whoever finds their life will lose it, and whoever loses their life for my sake will find it.

Wow, Jesus was very radical. It costs everything to follow Him.

After Jesus walked here on earth, preaching the Kingdom of God, and performing many signs and wonders, He died on a cross for you and me so that we could live. And because Jesus died on the cross, everything changed. Jesus paid the price for our sins so that we could go free. We read some of what Jesus endured before He was crucified in Matthew 27:28-31, which states:

They stripped him and put a scarlet robe on him, and then twisted together a crown of thorns and set it on his head. They put a staff in his right hand. Then they knelt in front of him and mocked him. "Hail, king of the Jews!" they said. They spit on him, and took the staff and struck him on the head again and again. After they had mocked him, they took off the robe and put his own clothes on him. Then they led him away to crucify him.

When they crucified Him, they hung Him on a cross, and while He was hanging there, before He died, we read, in Matthew 27:46, *"About three in the afternoon Jesus cried out in a loud voice, "Eli, Eli, lema sabachthani?"(which means "My God, my God, why have you forsaken me?")*. We then read, in Matthew 27:50, *"And when Jesus had cried out again in a loud voice, he gave up his spirit."* And, as recorded in John 19:30, before Jesus took His last breath, He shouted, *"... It is finished...".* After Jesus gave up His Spirit, we read about how the temple veil, separating people from God, was torn in two. Wow, what an amazing moment! If we continue to read, we will see how Jesus was buried, but because Jesus was without sin, death could not hold Him, so He rose and conquered death. Yes, he paid the price for our sins, died on the cross and defeated death.

1 Corinthians 15:1-4 states:

Now, brothers and sisters, I want to remind you of the gospel I preached to you, which you received and on which you have taken your stand. By this gospel you are saved, if you hold firmly to the word I preached to you. Otherwise, you have believed in vain. For what I received I passed on to you as of first importance: that Christ died for our sins according to the Scriptures, that he was buried, that he was raised on the third day according to the Scriptures...

Hallelujah! This is amazing. And after Jesus rose from the grave, we read how He went to see his disciples. Jesus told his disciples, before he died on the cross and rose, to stay in Jerusalem until the promise of the Holy Spirit was fulfilled. And we read about this promise in Acts 1:4, which states, *"On one occasion, while he was eating with them, he gave them this command: 'Do not leave Jerusalem, but wait for the gift my Father promised, which you have heard me speak about.' "* After Jesus rose from the grave and appeared to His disciples, He went to heaven and sent His Holy Spirit down to earth.

THE GOOD NEWS

Today, because of what Jesus did for us, we can experience a new life – an eternal life. Yes, because of what He did, we can experience forgiveness for our sins. Jesus, in John 14:6, states, *"... I am the way and the truth and the life. No one comes to the Father except through me."* Yes, He made a way for us to be forgiven and reconciled to God. Jesus fulfilled the law of God and took the wrath of God upon Him by dying on the cross. But it is not enough that Jesus died on the cross for you if you don't receive it. You need to receive the message of the Gospel and act on it. Yes, you need to receive Jesus, repent, get baptized in water, and receive His Holy Spirit.

So Jesus is the answer to the problem of sin and what He did on the cross for us is the good news of the Gospel for us and all future generations to come. Romans 1:16 states, "For I am not ashamed of the gospel, because it is the power of God that brings salvation to everyone who believes: first to the Jew, then to the Gentile." After the Holy Spirit came over the first disciples, Peter and the other disciples stood up and said, in Acts 2:36-38:

Therefore let all Israel be assured of this: God has made this Jesus, whom you crucified, both Lord and Messiah. When the people heard this, they were cut to the heart and said to Peter and the other apostles, "Brothers, what shall we do?" Peter replied, "Repent and be baptized, every one of you, in the name of Jesus Christ for the forgiveness of your sins. And you will receive the gift of the Holy Spirit.

Amen! As this verse says, today, we need to repent, be baptized in water, and receive the Holy Spirit. We need to recognize that we have sinned against a holy and righteous God. But if we do not see that we have sinned against God, we will not change and repent, and we will not experience forgiveness. We need to repent. Mark 1:15 states, " *'The time has come,' he said. 'The kingdom of God has come near. Repent and believe the good news!' "* When we turn away from our sins and put our faith in Jesus, God will come and give us a new heart. We see this in Ezekiel 36:26, which states, " *I will give you a new heart and put a new spirit in you; I will remove from you your heart of stone and give you a heart of flesh."*

So believe in Jesus, repent of your sins, and God will forgive you and cleanse you from all unrighteousness. And like Jesus says, in Mark 16:16, we must also be baptized in water, as it states, *"Whoever believes and is baptized will be saved, but whoever does not believe will be condemned."* Acts 2:41 continues to talk about baptism through stating, *"Those who accepted his message were baptized, and about three thousand were added to their number that day."* In water baptism, we die with Christ, burying our sins, and rise with Christ, set free from the slavery of sin. Baptism is absolutely necessary to follow Jesus. But you also need to receive the

Holy Spirit. Jesus spoke about how He would send down His Holy Spirit to earth in John14:26, which states, *"But the Advocate, the Holy Spirit, whom the Father will send in my name, will teach you all things and will remind you of everything I have said to you."* People often receive the Holy Spirit by having other people with the Spirit pray for them. And we can read how Peter and John, in Acts 8, laid hands on the believers there in Samaria and how they received the Holy Spirit. We can also read about how Paul, in Acts 19, laid hands on the people in Ephesus and how they received the Holy Spirit, spoke in tongues and prophesied. And this is how it should still be today.

I have prayed for hundreds of people who have received the Holy Spirit. If you don't receive the Holy Spirit right away after you are baptized, don't give up. Keep praying for God to give you His Spirit. When we receive the Holy Spirit, we become part of the body of Christ and Jesus is the head. And when we become part of the body of Christ, our mission on earth is to continue to do what Jesus started. Jesus, when He sent out His disciples, said in Matthew 10:7-8, *"As you go, proclaim this message: 'The kingdom of heaven has come near.' Heal the sick, raise the dead, cleanse those who have leprosy, drive out demons. Freely you have received; freely give."* These words that Jesus spoke to His disciples are so important for us, as this is what we are still called to do today.

A NEW BEGINNING

One day, Jesus will return to judge the world and make everything good and perfect again. And we who are born again will be able to eat from the Tree of Life and live forever. But in order to partake of the Tree of Life, we must believe in Jesus, repent, be baptized in water, and receive the Holy Spirit. And after this, we must continue walking with Him for the rest of our lives. We see that we must always continue to follow Jesus in Matthew 24:13-14, which states, *"... But the one who stands firm to the end will be saved. And this gospel of the kingdom will be preached in the whole world as a testimony to all nations, and then the end will come."* Yes, if we stand firm to the end, we will be saved. When Jesus comes back, He will judge the world and divide His sheep from the goats. And as we read in Hebrew 9:27-28, *"Just as people are destined to die once, and after that to face judgment, so Christ was sacrificed once to take away the sins of many; and he will appear a second time, not to bear sin, but to bring salvation to those who are waiting for him."* Yes, we will all die and face judgment, and Jesus will gather every nation to separate His people from the people of the world like a shepherd separates the sheep from the goats. And in the last book of the Bible, Revelation, we read about how God will come down to earth with the new Jerusalem. Revelation 22:3-5 states:

No longer will there be any curse. The throne of God and of the Lamb will be in the city, and his servants will serve him. They will see his face, and his name will be on their foreheads. There will be no more night. They will not need the light of a lamp or the light of the sun, for the Lord God will give them light. And they will reign for ever and ever.

And Revelation 22:14 continues to state, *"Blessed are those who wash their robes, that they may have the right to the tree of life and may go through the gates into the city."* Amen!

So to summarize, God created a perfect world, but sin came in through one man, Adam. And because of sin, man was banished from the garden of Eden, away from the Tree of Life. And this was very important so that man could not eat of that tree and live forever. Death came to all men because all have sinned. And Jesus came as the new Adam to save us from our sins. He paid the price by dying on the cross, and because He was without sin, He rose, sent down His Holy Spirit to earth, and is now sitting beside God's right hand. One day, He will come back and judge both the dead and the living. Those who have washed their robes by the blood of Jesus (those who have repented, got baptized in water, received the Holy Spirit, and got born again) will be able to enter the new Jerusalem and eat from the Tree of Life and live forever.

I want to end off by saying that it is not enough for you to hear, read, or dream about this. No, you need to experience it. If you are not born again, repent and ask people around you to help baptize you in water and pray for you to receive the Holy Spirit. It is your life and your decision, but we are here to help you.

QUESTIONS & ANSWERS

HELP THEM TO MAKE THE DECISION

In this lesson, we have taken time to share the full Gospel with you and this is the responsibility that we, as believers, have. Yes, we have the responsibility to share the truth – the whole truth. Paul, in Acts 20:26-27 states, *"Therefore, I declare to you today that I am innocent of the blood of any of you."* Why did Paul say this? He said this because he realized the responsibility, given to him by God, to share the whole truth and this is what He did.

Imagine you see a burning house and a man trapped inside. You would be responsible to try and help the man to get out. Yes, if you see someone who is in a life or death situation, you would be responsible to try and help them and if you didn't try to do something to help them, you would be held accountable and found guilty of committing a crime before the court. In the same way, the Bible says that we have a responsibility to share the whole truth, and if we don't, we will be held accountable before God. So Paul knew the scriptures and knew what Ezekiel 3 said. Ezekiel 3:18-20 states:

When I say to a wicked person, 'You will surely die,' and you do not warn them or speak out to dissuade them from their evil ways in order to save their life, that wicked person will die for their sin, and I will hold you accountable for their blood. But if you do warn the wicked person and they do not turn from their wickedness or from their evil ways, they will die for their sin; but you will have saved yourself. "Again, when a righteous person turns from their righteousness and does evil, and I put a stumbling block before them, they will die. Since you did not warn them, they will die for their sin. The righteous things that person did will not be remembered, and I will hold you accountable for their blood.

Wow, this is strong. And because Paul knew this, he knew that he was obligated to tell people the truth. He understood that the peoples' blood would be on his hands if he did not preach the whole truth to them. And that is why, in Acts 20:26-27, we read, *"Therefore, I declare to you today that I am innocent of the blood of any of you. For I have not hesitated to proclaim to you the whole will of God."* So he could say that he was innocent because he spoke the whole will of God. If Paul would have hesitated and not preached the Gospel, he would not be able to say that he was innocent of the blood of those people.

Our responsibility is to preach the whole truth. That is our job. The job of the people who hear the truth is to receive the truth and repent. And when you share the Gospel with someone, you need to help them to choose. You need to make it clear to them, that now they have heard the truth, that they must decide what they want to do in response to it. Help them to understand that today is the day of salvation and that the choice of life and death has been put before them and that they are free to choose. We, as believers, need to be better at asking people, "What will you do about what you have heard? Do you want to repent and follow Christ? Yes or no?" Yes, ask them this question and if they say, "No," that's fine. They made their choice. But something amazing I have seen is that when people say, "No," that the Holy Spirit often starts to work in them. Yes, they may leave you and think, "Whoa, I just said no. Am I sure? What if I am making a mistake?" And they may actually return to you and yes, "Yes, I want to follow Jesus."

So It is important to ask them what they want to do. If they say, "Yes," then you can tell them, "That's great. Start with going to talk to God. It is God that you have sinned against and it is God that you need to repent towards. Ask God to come and show you your sins." We often pray together with people when they decide they want to repent and follow Jesus. And we often lead them through a prayer, where they say, "God, please show me my sins. Help me to see what I have done wrong against you. Help me to see my sins so that I can repent of them." And then you can let the Holy Spirit work and reveal their sins to them so that they can repent. I often also tell people, "Ok, now that you have heard the Gospel and have decided to follow Jesus, go for a ten minute walk and tell God that you are sorry for your sins. Ask God to forgive you of your sins and tell Him that you want to follow Him." Then, let them have some time alone to grieve over their sins, to think about what they have done against God, and to repent. And when they return, baptize them in water to Jesus Christ, and pray for them to receive the Holy Spirit.

Be bold. After people have seen this lesson in the **Kickstart Package**, ask each of them, "What do you want to do with what you have heard? Do you want to repent, turn away from your sins, be baptized to Christ, and follow Him? Yes or no?" And then let people give you an answer. This is so important. If people say that they cannot choose right away, that is fine. Tell them that they can give you a yes or no answer the next day. If we start to do this, we will see so many more people to Christ. Why? Well, because many people hear the Gospel and think, "Yes, I think I want to follow Jesus, but I will let God come and save me. I'll wait for Him." But when you ask them what they are going to do with what they have heard, it will help them to understand that, now they have heard the truth, it is not God's responsibility to do something, but theirs. It is not God's turn to move. No, they need to repent, get baptized to Jesus and receive His Holy Spirit.

WHY DID GOD PUT THE TREE OF KNOWLEDGE OF GOOD AND EVIL IN THE GARDEN OF EDEN?

This is a great question. To answer this question, it is important to compare the garden of Eden (at the beginning of the Bible) to the garden mentioned in Revelation (at the end of the Bible). In the beginning of Genesis, we see that there was the Tree of Life and the Tree of Knowledge of Good and Evil. Revelation 22 speaks about a new garden where there is no Tree of Knowledge of Good and Evil, but only the Tree of Life. Why was the Tree of Knowledge of Good and Evil in the beginning, but not in the end? Well, this is because God wants us to have free will – He wants us to be able to choose freely. He wants real love, real commitment, and a real relationship with us, but He gave us the choice to choose if we wanted to accept Him or deny Him. Throughout the Bible, we see how there is always a choice between life (the narrow road) and death (the broad road). God put these choices in front us of so that we could decide. What will you decide? Will you choose life or death? Will you choose sin or righteousness? Will you choose to walk by the flesh or by the Spirit? Galatians 5:16 states, *"So I say, walk by the Spirit, and you will not gratify the desires of the flesh."*

So in the garden of Eden, there was the Tree of Knowledge of Good and Evil and the Tree of Life because God wanted them to have the choice from what tree they wanted to eat from. But in the new heaven and new earth, God is going to gather all of His people who have already chosen Him in this life. Yes, He will gather all of the people who have already chosen life, righteousness, and Him and He will put us in the new garden. And the Tree of Knowledge of Good and Evil will not be there because the people there have already made their choice in this life to choose Him.

The Tree of Life is a symbol of Christ and the Tree of Knowledge of Good and Evil is a symbol of this world and what it has to offer us. If you, in this life, choose Christ, then you will enter the new heaven and new earth.

When I talk about my wife, I know that she loves me. Why? Well, because she has chosen to be with me. And I love my wife and she knows that because I have chosen to be with her. If she did not have a choice and was forced to marry me, how can I be sure that she loves me? How could I be sure if she didn't have free will and was forced to be with me? And it is the same with God. He wants to give us free will and for us to choose to love Him and choose to be with Him.

CAN YOU LOSE YOUR SALVATION? WHAT ABOUT ONCE SAVED, ALWAYS SAVED?

There is a popular teaching going around in many church denominations saying "once saved, always saved." A big problem with this view is how people look at salvation. We are not already saved, as we are not yet standing in the new heaven and new earth with access to the Tree of Life. We are still here on earth. When we read about salvation in the Bible, it is always referred to in past, present, and future tense. Yes, we were saved because of what Jesus did, we are getting saved because God is working in us, and the Bible says, in Matthew 24:13, *"But he who endures to the end shall be saved."* And Paul, in 1 Corinthians 9:24, states, *"Do you not know that those who run in a race all run, but one receives the prize? Run in such a way that you may obtain it."* So we read here that we must run the race to obtain eternal life. Paul, in 1 Corinthians 9:27, also states, *"But I discipline my body and bring it into subjection, lest, when I have preached to others, I myself should become disqualified."* So we must run and not get disqualified, as when one gets disqualified, they are out of the race. It is clear that these verses are talking about salvation.

In 1 Corinthians 10, we read about how the Israelites where saved out of Egypt by the blood, then how they were saved from their sin through the baptism to Moses and then, how they were supposed to walk under the cloud. But we read that many of them did not enter the promise land and were killed in the desert. We read about these things in 1 Corinthians 10:1-5, which states:

Moreover, brethren, I do not want you to be unaware that all our fathers were under the cloud, all passed through the sea, all were baptized into Moses in the cloud and in the sea, all ate the same spiritual food, and all drank the same spiritual drink. For they drank of that spiritual Rock that followed them, and that Rock was Christ. But with most of them God was not well pleased, for their bodies were scattered in the wilderness.

And then we read this 1 Corinthians 10:11 that everything that happened to them was written down as a warning for us so we should not do like that:

So if we look at salvation we are not once saved always saved yet. But if we continue in Christ and not like we read about a branch that does not bear fruit he cuts it off and throw it away, but if we continue to let God change us and continue abiding in Christ, we one day will be saved – once saved always saved. But until that time, we are not. Some would then quote Romans 8:35-39 (NKJV) which states,

Who shall separate us from the love of Christ? Shall tribulation, or distress, or persecution, or famine, or nakedness, or peril, or sword? As it is written: "FOR YOUR SAKE WE ARE KILLED ALL DAY LONG; WE ARE ACCOUNTED AS SHEEP FOR THE SLAUGHTER." Yet in all these things we are more than conquerors through Him who loved us. For I am persuaded that neither death nor life, nor angels nor principalities nor powers, nor things present nor things to come, nor height nor depth, nor any other created thing, shall be able to separate us from the love of God which is in Christ Jesus our Lord.

If you look at that list, there is one thing that is not written in that list and that is yourself. Yes, nothing from the outside can steal your salvation. So no, the Bible is not giving us a once saved always saved on this side of eternity, but when we are on the other side in the new Jerusalem and eating of the Tree of Life where there will be no more tears Revelations 21: 2-4 and there we will be once saved always saved.

The Bible makes it clear that we can lose our salvation. But I don't believe that we lose it in a matter of a day. No, but we can lose it if we continue living in sin and disobedience.

And God does not strike a man forever and we can sin against what the Bible says, the Holy Spirit. What we see in the Bible is that all sin committed against Jesus will experience forgiveness, but Jesus said in Matthew 12:30-32 (NKJV)the one who sins against the Holy Spirit shall not be forgiven:

He who is not with Me is against Me, and he who does not gather with Me scatters abroad. "Therefore I say to you, every sin and blasphemy will be forgiven men, but the blasphemy against the Spirit will not be forgiven men. Anyone who speaks a word against the Son of Man, it will be forgiven him; but whoever speaks against the Holy Spirit, it will not be forgiven him, either in this age or in the age to come.

What is it to sin against the Holy Spirit? Hebrews 10:26 and on is very scary, but this is a reality. The Bible says that, "*for if we sin willfully after we have received the knowledge of the truth, there no longer remains a sacrifice for sins, but a certain fearful expectation of judgment, and fiery indignation which will devour the adversaries. Anyone who has rejected Moses' law dies without mercy on the testimony of two or three witnesses*".

This is scary but we need to understand that God is also a consuming fire in the new testament. We need to understand that those who sinned under Moses there was a punishment, but we also read how much harder will the punishment not be if we have sinned and trampled the son of God under foot. What does that mean? If we go back in the beginning, the Bible says if you sin willfully after you have received the knowledge of the truth and experienced the power of the one to come. In Christ there is freedom. In Christ, when you are fully born again there is freedom from sin. If you then after being washed free and after experiencing the power of the world to come and then go back sinning willfully or living in sin, you can not only lose your salvation, but you can also come to a point where you cannot find salvation again. And that is scary to think of but that is what we need to preach because this is what the Bible says. Hebrews 6 is saying the same about someone who falls away – there is no way back. The Bible also said in 2 Peter 2:21 -22, the one who has tasted this and fall away is like the dog going back to the vomit.

What we need is the fear of God. We need to understand the reality of the world we are living in. We in the church have seen many people come to Christ, fall away, come back to Christ, go back in sin and go back to Christ. And then people say, but how can we explain that when the Bible comes with very clear verses here that if you keep on going there could be a place where there is no way back. The answer is that many of those people who were in church and fell away have never really experienced the knowledge of the truth, never really experienced the power of the world to come, never really experienced the freedom from sin and they have been overcome by sin and they have never experienced the freedom and then the old life can and took over again. Can they come back to Christ? Of course. Because they have not fully been in Him in the first place. But for those who fully are in Him and experienced the world and life to come, for us, we cannot just keep going on in our sins. We cannot keep sinning willfully. We cannot live in it because then we will not only lose our salvation, we will also experience a place where we can not come back to God. I wrote a whole book about this called "The Sound Doctrine" where I talk about the fear of God and how we need to understand the seriousness of sin and what Jesus came to do, how He came to set us free and I recommend that book for everyone who wants to go deeper into this.

So can you lose your salvation? Not in that sense where one day you wake up and you are lost, not in that sense that you have fallen in sin one day and done something wrong because 1 John 1:9 states, *if we confess our sins, He is faithful and just to forgive us our sins and to cleanse us from all unrighteousness.* But if you continue in your sins, if you don't listen to the Spirit that is teaching you and wanting you to depart from evilness and is saying to you don't go back to sin, if you don't listen to the Holy Spirit in what He is teaching you. Therefore, you are sinning against the Spirit of Christ and yes then you can not only lose your salvation, but you can actually experience reaching a point where the Spirit doesn't strive with man forever and you will not be able to come back to God. So like Paul wrote in Corinthians 9, let's take care of our bodies, let's go into strict training, let's run the race in front of us so we do not only start this race but finish it, complete it and get the crown of righteousness God calls everyone to.

WHY IS JESUS REFERRED TO AS THE NEW ADAM?

In the beginning, God created man. Why? He created man because He wanted fellowship with man. He wanted man to take possession of this earth and He wanted to walk with man. But, as we have seen, sin came in and destroyed everything. So God, in the garden of Eden, already created a plan to save us. God, in Genesis 3:15 (NKJV) states, *"And I will put enmity between you and the woman, and between your seed and her Seed; He shall bruise your head, and you shall bruise His heel."* This "seed" God is referring to is Jesus. Yes, God is talking about the seed born of a virgin woman that will later come to save His people from their sins and that is Jesus Christ.

Romans 5:12 states, *"Therefore, just as through one man's sin entered the world, and death through sin, and thus death spread to all men, because all sinned—..."*. John 10:10 states, *"... I have come that they may have life, and that they may have it more abundantly."* So Christ is referred to as the second Adam, as He came to undo the fall of man caused by Adam and Eve. 1 Corinthians 15:22 (NKJV) states, *"For as in Adam all die, even so in Christ all shall be made alive."* So all were condemned through Adam because we have all, like Adam, sinned. John 3:17 (NKJV)states, *"For God did not send His Son into the world to condemn the world, but that the world through Him might be saved."* So Jesus came to restore what was broken in the garden of Eden. 1 Corinthians 15:45 (NKJV) states, *"And so it is written, 'The first man Adam became a living being.' The last Adam became a life-giving spirit."* So we can see, from these verses, that Jesus is referred to as the new Adam.

KNOWING GOD

LESSON FIVE

Welcome to **Lesson Five** of this **Kickstart Package**. In this lesson, I will be sharing about knowing God. So far, I have talked about discipleship, the Gospel, and how to be born again. I hope you who are reading this book have come to faith in Jesus, repented, been baptized in water, and received the Holy Spirit. If you have done this, congratulations! You are now born again! You are a new creation. The old you has gone, and something new has begun. Welcome to a new and amazing life with God.

2 Corinthians 5:17 (NIV), states, *"Therefore, if anyone is in Christ, the new creation has come: The old has gone, the new is here!"* As we can see from this verse, when we are born again, old things have passed away, and something new has begun. If we continue reading in this biblical passage, we can see how God reconciles us through Jesus Christ and through Him has given us the ministry of reconciliation. So, we are now called to reconcile people back to God. We can see this in 2 Corinthians 5:20, as it talks about how we are ambassadors of Christ. It states, *"We are therefore Christ's ambassadors, as though God were making his appeal through us. We implore you on Christ's behalf: Be reconciled to God."*

Now that you have received a new life with Jesus, you have a new job. You are now here on earth as Christ's ambassador to represent Him and reconcile people back to God. You will need time to learn and to grow as a disciple/apprentice of

TO WALK LIKE HIM

TO TALK LIKE HIM

TO BE LED BY THE HOLY SPIRIT LIKE HIM

TO HEAL THE SICK CAST OUT DEMONS LIKE HIM

Jesus. Yes, we all need time to learn how to represent Jesus here on earth. We all need to learn how to walk, talk, be led by the Holy Spirit, share the Gospel, heal the sick, and cast out demons like Jesus. We truly have so much to learn from Him.

Discipleship is so important, and it is helpful to walk with other disciples of Jesus because we can learn from one another. However, our most important relationship is with God. Everything we do should be a result of our relationship with Him. It's important that we know and love Him and, therefore, obey Him. I still remember the first time I experienced God. Everything was so new to me. At the time, I knew God existed, but I did not know who He was. I remember looking up into the sky and saying that God (or whoever was there) should come and take me, expecting a UFO to come and beam me up. I really did not know God like I do today.

Over the last 23 years, I have grown a lot in my relationship with God, and He still continues to teach me. I have experienced God doing amazing things through me. Serving Him is amazing, and it is not work. It is life. There is nothing better than walking with God and being used by Him. Ephesians 2:8-9 states, *"For it is by grace you have been saved, through faith—and this is not from yourselves, it is the gift of God—not by works, so that no one can boast."* We are saved through faith in Jesus Christ, and this is a gift from God. The next verse, Ephesians 2:10 (NKJV), states, *"For we are His workmanship, created in Christ Jesus for good works, which God prepared beforehand that we should walk in them."* So we are not saved by works, but we are saved and given an amazing life filled with the good works God has prepared for us to walk in. As 2 Corinthians 5:20 tells us, we are here as Christ's ambassadors to walk in the amazing things He has created for us to walk in.

Many years ago, I was seeking God and fasting when I heard God speak to me. I heard God say, "Go to Nakskov." It's a city in Denmark located about four and a half hours away from where my family and I lived at the time. When I heard this, I questioned why God wanted me to go there. I knew, however, that He had told me to go there, so I said to my wife, Lene, "We need to go to Nakskov. God just told me we need to go." So we drove to the city, and when we arrived, I prayed and said to God, "Ok, God, I am here now. I know You want me to be here. I heard You clearly say that this is where You wanted me to go. But now that I have arrived, what should I do?" After spending a few days in the city, I met a man who had a problem with his knee, and he asked me if I could pray for him. He also told me he needed to have an operation on his knee the next day. So, I prayed for him, and God completely healed his knee. He walked up and down the stairs to test his knee out, and he no longer had any problems with it. He was so thankful and told me he was going to cancel his operation that was scheduled for the next day. Then he looked at me and said something that changed my life. He asked me, "Torben, when did God speak to you about coming to Nakskov?" I looked at him confused and asked, "What?" He asked me again, and I answered, "Uhm... Thursday at three o'clock while I was praying. Why are you asking?" He then shared how he heard about me on Monday and began praying from Monday until Wednesday that God would send me to his city so that I could pray for him to be healed. When I heard this, I was shocked.

It was amazing to think about how I met a man on the other side of Denmark who had been praying for three days for me to go to his city so I could pray for him to be healed. It was incredible to think about how God, on Thursday, told me to go to Nakskov, and then I met the man on Sunday, the day before his operation. When I experienced this, I became so excited because I knew I was walking in something God had prepared for me to walk in. I realized God had organized this meeting before I was even created, and that He planned to use me to heal this man. I realized I was here on earth to represent Him as the body of Christ, and to be led by His Holy Spirit. When I experienced this, I knew I wanted more. From that point on, I continued to grow with God, listen to His voice, and experience more and more amazing things. This life is for you, too. Are you ready to follow Jesus as His disciple? Are you ready to represent Him on earth, follow His voice, and walk in what He has prepared for you?

In order to understand how to know God and listen to His voice, we need to look at the Bible. Oftentimes, God speaks to us through His Word (the Bible). The Bible is not like any other book. It is a life-changing book, full of truth. When we get born again and receive the Holy Spirit, the Holy Spirit will help us to understand the Bible. The Holy Spirit is our Helper, and He teaches us the truth that sets us free. In John 14:26 (NIV), Jesus says, *"But the Advocate, the Holy Spirit, whom the Father will send in My name, will teach you all things and will remind you of everything I have said to you."*

God often speaks to us through His Word. In Luke 24, we read about how Jesus, after He rose again, met two of his disciples on the way to a small village called Emmaus. He approached the disciples and started to walk and talk with them, but He kept His identity a secret from them. We read how, while they were walking and talking on the way to Emmaus, they spoke about what had happened in Jerusalem, about Jesus and how He had died, and about the empty grave. Jesus, still hiding His identity, followed them to their home and broke bread with all of His disciples. Suddenly, they recognized that it was Jesus. When they saw it was Jesus, He disappeared. The disciples, in Luke 24:32, asked each other, *"... Were not our hearts burning within us while He talked with us on the road and opened the Scriptures to us?"* This "burning" the disciples spoke about here is something you can experience in your heart today when you walk with Jesus. You can experience the Holy Spirit revealing Scripture to you, and the Word of God becoming so real to you that you can feel it burning in your heart, just like the disciples did.

There have been many times that I have experienced a burning inside of me while reading the Bible. The Word of God becomes alive inside me, and I can feel it in my heart. If you don't have the Holy Spirit, you will not experience this. Without the Spirit of God, the Bible will be like every other book—powerless. With the Holy Spirit, God will speak to you through His Word, and it will be powerful. God can also speak directly to us through visions, dreams, and a little voice inside of us.

THE SPIRIT

VISIONS,
DREAMS,
LITTLE VOICE
INSIDE OF US
...

THE BIBLE

WE RENEW OUR
MIND TO KNOW
GOD'S WILL,
WE TEST

We are called to walk with God. In order to walk, we need both of our legs. Spiritually speaking, the first leg is the Word of God (the Bible), and the second leg is the Holy Spirit. Romans 12:1-2 (NIV) states:

Therefore, I urge you, brothers and sisters, in view of God's mercy, to offer your bodies as a living sacrifice, holy and pleasing to God—this is your true and proper worship. Do not conform to the pattern of this world, but be transformed by the renewing of your mind. Then you will be able to test and approve what God's will is—His good, pleasing and perfect will.

From this verse, we see that we can renew our mind through the Word of God, and use it to know God's will for our lives. It is important to use the Word of God to test things, to see whether or not what we heard is from God.

After Jesus got baptized, He went out into the desert for forty days and forty nights and was tempted by Satan. There in the desert, Satan used Bible verses out of context to try and trick Jesus into sin. However, Jesus knew the Word better than Satan and answered him with the Word of God. Eventually, Satan left Him. Today, Satan still tries to trick disciples of Jesus by using Bible verses out of context. As disciples, we will also experience attacks like Jesus did in the desert. Satan will come and try to deceive us. He can attack us through speaking directly to us, using the Word of God out of context, or through other people's words.

I would like to share a testimony about how strong and real attacks from Satan can be. First, I would like to start off by sharing about one of the first times I really experienced hearing from God. This is when I first met my wife. At that time, I was only a Christian for a few months. I was attending a large Christian concert when I suddenly heard God say, "Torben, the girl standing behind you is going to be your wife." Instantly, I knew it was God who had just spoken to me. I was so excited and thought, *Whoa, my wife is standing behind me!* I turned around and quickly looked at her and thought, *Whoa, that is my wife!* Despite there being about 500 hundred people at the concert, when I turned around and saw the young woman standing a little farther down the aisle, I just knew God was talking about her. I smiled at her, but I had to hurry home after the concert and did not have the opportunity to talk to her. On my way home, I said to my friend, Michael, "I just saw my wife! I don't know her name, her age, or where she's from, but God told me she's going to be my wife." I thanked God for the young woman who was going to be my wife, and I thanked Him because I knew He would bring us together. Three months later, God put us together. Today, at the time of this writing, we have been married for 24 years and have three children and two grandchildren. It is truly such an amazing story.

Some years later, I experienced something that might sound weird to people who don't know the spiritual world. I suddenly experienced an attack. I began hearing a voice saying, "Leave your wife, leave your kids, and go out into the world." I was shocked when I heard it. And again, I heard, "Leave your wife, leave your kids, and go out into the world." The voice was very real, but because I knew the Scriptures and had the Word of God inside of me, I knew that this voice was not from God. So, I went for a walk and prayed, "Go away, in the name of Jesus! Satan, I command you to leave me alone, in the name of Jesus! I am not going to leave my wife, I am not going to leave my kids, and I am not going to go out into the world! I love you, Jesus, I love my wife, and I love my kids." As I was praying, I was fighting and standing firm on the Word of God. But that voice persisted in my head for three days. After three days, it suddenly left. I was confused and thought, "What just happened?" Later, God showed me that I had been under a strong spiritual attack from our enemy. After that attack, I experienced an even greater breakthrough in my life.

God can speak to us, and so can our enemy. This is why it is so important to test everything we hear with the Word of God. We must have the Word of God inside us so that we can discern if it is our own thought, a lie from Satan, or truth from God. We must read the Word of God from the beginning to the end, chapter by chapter. We need to meditate and reflect on the verses. When the Word of God is inside us, it will be much easier to know God's will, discern His voice, overcome sin, and much more. We need to spend time with God. It takes time to really get to know God's voice.

Since I have been walking with God for many years, it has become much easier for me to recognize His voice. However, when I was young in the faith, it was very hard for me to hear from God. I remember feeling so frustrated because I thought God was speaking to every Christian except me. One time, I went out for a walk in the forest, and I began to pray. I felt so frustrated and said, "God, why don't You speak to me? I read in Your Word that Your sheep hear Your voice, and that You speak to those who belong to You. So why don't You speak to me? What's wrong with me? Why can't I hear Your voice?" As I continued walking and praying, I saw some people working in the forest. I ignored them and continued to pray. Suddenly, I had the thought, "Go and speak to them about God." I assumed it was just my own thoughts, so I ignored it and continued on, saying, "God, why don't You speak to me?" Once again, I heard, "Go and speak to them about God." But again, I believed I was hearing my own voice, so I continued to ignore it. As I started to pray and once more ask God why He didn't speak to me, I again had the thought to go and talk to the people about God. Why did I continue thinking it was just my thoughts and not God speaking to me? Well, because I did not hear a loud voice. I only received a small thought. So, I kept praying, but the thought remained in my head. I then stopped praying and asked, "God, is this you? Or is it just my own thoughts?" I decided that the only way to know if it was God or not was to test it out. So, I turned around and went back to the people working in the forest. I remember feeling so nervous. I approached them and timidly asked, "Excuse me, do you have five minutes?" I then quickly began to tell them about how I met God, and then I thanked them, said goodbye, and left.

As I walked away, I thought I must not have heard from God because nothing amazing happened when I told them about Him. However, one week later, a woman approached me and said, "Hello, Torben." She then took my hand and thanked me profusely. I was confused and asked her why she was thanking me. She began telling me how thankful she was because her brother was falling away from Christ, and she and her family had been praying for him. She told me that last week, he was out working in a forest, and I had approached him and spoke directly into his life, and that now, he has come back to God. When I heard this, everything changed. As she stood there thanking me, and telling me this story, I understood that it was God who had spoken to me, that the thought I had received while praying in the forest was not my own thought. It was God speaking to me and leading me by His Holy Spirit. I realized then that I had been there in that forest to represent Him on earth, and that I was walking in what God had prepared for me to do. I was so amazed that the voice of God was only a small thought in my head and not a loud voice saying, "This is God!"

I began to realize that if God speaks to me through little thoughts, maybe He has spoken to me many times, but I had not listened because I was expecting to hear a loud voice. From that moment on, I tried to pay attention to this more, and whenever I got a thought in my head like, *Go and say something to that person, Go and pray for that person's knee, Send flowers to that person, or Call that person and tell them what I have told you*, I started to do it. And when I approached someone and said, "Excuse me, do you have pain in your shoulder?" and they did, they were shocked. I was able to tell them that God had told me, and then I prayed for them. When I asked if someone had pain in a specific part of their body and was wrong, I would realize that it was just my own thought. By doing this again and again, it started to become easier and easier for me to recognize when I heard my own thought or when I heard from God.

Imagine your telephone is ringing, and you don't recognize the number. You pick it up and say, "Hello?" If someone you know very well is calling you, they can just say, "Hey, it's me," and you will recognize who is calling right away. If someone knows me well, I don't need to say, "Hello, this is Torben Søndergaard from The Last Reformation." Why? Well, because if you've spent a lot of time with someone, you will recognize their voice right away. This is how it needs to be with God. We need to spend time with Him and listen to Him. Over time, it will become easier to recognize when God speaks to us, when Satan speaks to us, or when it is our own thoughts. I really want to encourage you to spend time with God and try to listen to Him.

Prayer is not what many people think it is. Many people think they need to pray at a certain time every day, or when they lie down to go to sleep at night. However, prayer is life. In prayer, we share everything with God. It can be when we are out driving, walking, or when we are alone, kneeling down by our bed. God wants to have a relationship with us, and prayer is not bound to location or time. When you pray, share everything with God and then spend some time just listening to His voice. God desires to be part of your everyday life, and if you are born again, you belong to Him. Don't just go out and get a new job, buy a house, or marry someone without seeking God and what His will is. God can lead you if you seek Him. He can tell you what job to apply for, what house to purchase, and who to marry. He wants to lead you.

I would like to tell you a story about how God can speak to us and lead us. About three years ago, I needed to buy a new car. I did not have much time to look for a car. I needed to buy one that day. I began searching on the Internet but quickly felt overwhelmed. I did not even know where to start. As I was searching, I became confused and unsure about what car to get. I walked into a car dealership and saw a beautiful, white Peugeot. As I stood there in front of it, I thought to myself, Wow, this is a really nice car. I love this car. But, at the same time, I wasn't sure if it was the car God wanted me to get. I really wanted to buy the car God desired for me. Overwhelmed, I went home and began to pray. I said to God, "I need to buy a car today. What car do you want me to buy?" Suddenly, I got a thought. It was very clear but very confusing at the same time. I heard, "Go to the wedding." I was surprised and said, "What?" Again, I heard, "Go to the wedding."

In my city, on that day, a couple was getting married, but I decided to ignore the thought and not go because I didn't know them well and I had to purchase a car that day. So, I continued to pray and ask, "God, what car do I get?" Again, I heard, "Go to the wedding." I ignored the thought and said, "God I really need to find a car today. I don't have time to go to a wedding." But the thought persisted in my head, and even though I thought it was a bad idea, I knew if it was God speaking to me, then I needed to do it. So I told my wife, Lene, "I know we have guests coming over this afternoon, and I need to find a car today, and I know it seems like a bad idea, but I need to go to the wedding. I really believe God is telling me to go to the wedding." So, I got dressed up in nice clothes and drove to the wedding. As I was driving there, I was asking God, "Is this really You? I don't have time to go to a wedding today."

When I arrived at the wedding, I felt out of place and embarrassed because I hardly knew the couple getting married. When I walked in, a man greeted me and said, "Oh, Torben! Welcome. I'm surprised to see you here." *Yes, I am also surprised to be here*, I thought to myself. I was afraid everyone was looking at me and thinking *what is Torben doing here*? The ceremony started, and everyone was standing, worshipping God. As I was standing there, I was praying, "God, what am I doing here? I need a car today. What car do I get?" The couple got married, and it was a beautiful wedding. After the ceremony, I was sitting down eating some cake and drinking coffee, when suddenly an older man came and sat down beside me. We began to speak about God and the Holy Spirit, and while we were talking, someone came over and said to him, "Are you ready to leave in five minutes?" He replied, "I am ready to leave whenever they want me to leave." He began to tell me he was the wedding couple's chauffeur and that he was going to drive the couple out to take some wedding photos. Knowing that the tradition in Denmark is for the wedding couple to ask someone who has a nice car to be their chauffeur, I said, "You must have a nice car since they asked you." He looked at me and said, "Yes, young man." Then, he pointed his finger at me and said, "If you ever need to buy a new car, you need to buy a Toyota Advantis." Surprised, I replied, "Actually, I need to buy a new car today. Can we go out and look at your car?" He happily agreed, and together we went out to look at his car. It was a very nice car, newly washed and decorated with flowers for the wedding. As I stood there looking at the car, I thought, "Hmm... a Toyota Advantis. That is a nice car." But then I thought about the nice white Peugeot. I thought to myself, "But I like the Peugeot more." The man then placed his hand on my shoulder and said, "Young man, this is the best car I've ever had. It was not like the Peugeot I had before. That one always broke down. Never buy a Peugeot. You need to buy a Toyota Advantis." Shocked by his statement, I thought, *God, is this really You speaking to me?* Once more, the man put his hand on my shoulder and said, "So, young man, just listen to the Holy Spirit, you need to buy a Toyota Advantis."

That day, we bought a Toyota Advantis, and I knew it was God's will. It was so amazing to know God led me to that wedding where I met the man He used to speak to me three times. And even if any problems came with the Toyota Advantis, I knew God was in control. Why? Because it was His idea. He picked that car out for me. Of course, if you have a Peugeot, that is also a good car. However, God spoke very clearly, and I wanted to obey. God desires to lead us, He wants to speak to you, and He wants to be part of your life.

The last thing I want to talk about in this lesson is fellowship. Having fellowship with others is important. We learn to walk with God by spending time with others who are farther in their walk with God than we are. It is important to have other people around you to help you grow and learn to live the life God has for you. The Bible says we are all baptized into one body. We see this in 1 Corinthians 12:13 (NIV), which states, *"For we were all baptized by one Spirit so as to form one body—whether Jews or Gentiles, slave or free—and we were all given the one Spirit to drink."* So, we all make up one body, and we are all a family. When you get baptized, it is

not into a church organization or to a movement. It is into a family of brothers and sisters in Christ. The physical family includes parents, children, and babies, and it is the same in the Kingdom of God. In a fellowship of believers, there are babies, which represent people who are very new in their faith. There are children, which represent people who are a little stronger in their faith and have learned to walk with Jesus. And lastly, there are parents, which represent people who are mature and can spiritually support the younger ones. 1 John 2:12-13 talks about this by stating, *"I am writing to you, dear children, because your sins have been forgiven on account of His name. I am writing to you, fathers, because you know Him who is from the beginning. I am writing to you, young men, because you have overcome the evil one."* Here, we can see that John is writing to little children, young men, and fathers (otherwise referred to as babies, children, and parents).

When you get born again, you are like a baby in your faith, and babies need milk to grow. However, if you give milk to young men, they will not grow because they need solid food. It is the same way in the church. We all start off as babies, and we are dependent on other people around us to help us and teach us the truth. Then we grow up and learn to feed ourselves. At this point, we don't need much teaching from other people because we can read the Bible and understand it ourselves. As we continue to grow stronger and stronger, we become spiritual parents who help the next generation of disciples grow and mature. We need each other to grow, and it takes time.

As born-again believers, we have a ministry to reconcile people with God. We are put here on earth in Christ's place as ambassadors to represent Him and His Kingdom. To do this, we need to learn to walk with God. We need to read the Bible and meditate on the Word, so we know what the Word says. We need to learn to listen to God's Word, and we also need people around us who can help us, especially in the beginning. I hope this lesson has created a longing in you to experience this amazing life with God.

QUESTIONS & ANSWERS

HOW TO READ THE BIBLE

It is very important that we understand how to read the Bible correctly. The original text in the Bible was without chapters and verses. The books and letters were written as a whole and were not meant to be divided. It is important, when we want to study a subject in the Bible, to read the whole Bible and not just certain verses. When I say to "study a subject in the Bible," I am referring to how we, today, can buy a book written on, for example, the love of God. In books like this, we will find Bible verses talking about the love of God, and there's nothing wrong with that. We can also buy a book about the fear of God and find in that book Bible verses outlining how we are to fear and respect God. And there is also nothing wrong with that. However, when you read the whole Bible, you know you have received the whole truth and not just half-truths, which can sometimes happen when we read books about the Bible.

Unfortunately, many people today would rather read books about the Bible than to actually read the Bible itself. Because of this, people who read books about God's love think only that God is a loving God, while people who read books on God's wrath only think that God is a God of wrath. This can also happen when we hear teachings only on certain topics. Therefore, I encourage you to read the Bible book-by-book and letter-by-letter so you can understand all of Scripture in context.

It is also great to take different verses from the Bible and meditate on them. It is good to meditate on different verses you believe God wants to use to speak to you. We need to understand that faith comes by hearing by the Word of God. We see this in Romans 10:17 (NKJV), which states, *"So then faith comes by hearing, and hearing by the word of God"*. On the other hand, fear and doubts come by hearing things like the news. What you fill yourself with will determine if you are a person who walks in faith or in fear and doubt.

If you, for example, are experiencing an attack in your life, and you feel fear and doubt enter your mind, take the Word of God and fight. When you feel fear, quote the Word of God and say, for example, as stated in Matthew 6:26 (NKJV), *"Look at the birds of the air, for they neither sow nor reap nor gather into barns; yet your heavenly Father feeds them."* Or say, as Matthew 6:30 states, *"Now if God so clothes the grass of the field, which today is, and tomorrow is thrown into the oven, will He not much more clothe you, O you of little faith?"* God takes care of the birds and flowers so we know He will take care of us. You can also say, as stated in 1 John 4:18 (NIV), *"There is no fear in love. But perfect love drives out fear, because fear has to do with punishment. The one who fears is not made perfect in love."* Take the Word of God, meditate on it, speak it out, and believe it. When you do this, you will experience faith building up inside of you, and suddenly, the fear and doubt will disappear.

There have been many times in my life where fear and doubt came into my mind, and the Word of God helped me. For example, one time I went into the city to look for people to pray for. While I was there, I prayed for a young man with crutches, and he was completely healed. When he left, I watched him walk away carrying his crutches over his shoulder. As I turned around to walk away, I suddenly felt fear and doubt overwhelm me, and I heard, "God doesn't heal today." When I heard this, I was shocked and turned back around to see the young man carrying his crutches over his shoulder. And then again I heard, "God doesn't heal today." I continued to hear that thought, but I did not understand why because I knew that man was healed. Still, fear and doubt continued to persist in my mind. So, I took the Word of God and said, "No! Jesus said to go out and lay hands on the sick, and they shall recover. By His wounds, we are healed. Jesus commanded us in Luke 10:9 to go out and preach the Gospel and heal the sick." Suddenly, when I started to quote Bible verses, all the fear and doubt left me, and peace and faith came over me.

It is good to understand that faith comes by hearing the Word of God. It does not come by what we see or experience. What we see and experience can help create boldness in us, but it does not create faith. If I had not had the Word of God inside of me and had not taken the time to meditate on the verses and speak them out, I would not have had a weapon to use, to stand firm when the fear and doubt came.

I would like to tell you that I am not, and never have been a good reader, but thankfully, we live in a day and age where there are so many ways to receive the Word of God. So, if you do not like reading, you can also download the audio Bible on your phone and listen to it. I encourage you to find a way to hear or read the Word of God daily. The Word of God is our daily bread, and this is what our spirit needs to survive.

So, read the Word out loud, meditate on the verses, speak them out, write them down on a piece of paper, and listen to them throughout your day. There are so many ways to get the Word of God inside of us. It is important for your salvation and for you to finish the race. It is also important for you to be strong in the Word of God so you can help other believers around you.

CAN EVERYONE HEAR FROM GOD?

If you are born again, you can hear from God. Jesus stated in John 10:3 (NKJV), *"To him the doorkeeper opens, and the sheep hear his voice; and he calls his own sheep by name and leads them out."* Jesus uses this picture to show us that when we are born again, He is our Shepherd, and we are His sheep. Sheep know their shepherd's voice, just like we are to know the voice of our Shepherd, Jesus.

Yes, everyone who is born again can hear from God, but we need to learn to listen. I encourage you to take the time to listen and be quiet. Don't play the television or radio all day. Why? If you listen to a song and then shut off the radio, that song can still play over and over again in your head for quite some time. And if you have too many noises in your head and never take the time to be quiet and seek God, how can you hear Him? Romans 12:1 (NIV) states, *"Therefore, I urge you, brothers and sisters, in view of God's mercy, to offer your bodies as a living sacrifice, holy and pleasing to God—this is your true and proper worship."* And verse 2 states, *"Do not conform to the pattern of this world, but be transformed by the renewing of your mind. Then you will be able to test and approve what God's will is—his good, pleasing and perfect will."* The Bible says that we—you and I—need to offer our bodies as a sacrifice and to be transformed in our minds so that we will know the perfect will of God.

If you are born again, God is speaking to you, but He often doesn't speak to you as fast as you would like. It's not like you go into your bedroom, shut the door, and then immediately hear from God. We need to offer our bodies as a sacrifice to Him, to be transformed, and to seek Him. The Bible says in Matthew 7:7-8 (NIV), *"Ask and it will be given to you; seek and you will find; knock and the door will be opened to you. For everyone who asks receives; the one who seeks finds; and to the one who knocks, the door will be opened."* This verse is very interesting. It does not say to knock only once and the door will be opened, and it does not say to ask once and you will receive an answer. It also does not say to seek once and then you will find. It is clearly written that we need to keep asking, seeking, and knocking.

I have been following God for over 20 years, and it is very seldom that I go into my bedroom to pray and receive an answer from God immediately. Most times, I have to seek God for a long time, and then I will receive an answer. I know God is listening to me when I pray, and I seek Him even when I don't feel like He's listening. I remember when I used to wake up early every morning to go for a prayer walk. I used to pray the same thing every morning. I said, "God, use me. Please use me. God, send me. I will go where You want me to go. I will say what You want me to say. Please use me." I prayed this every morning for many months. At that time, I did not experience God speaking to me, and I did not feel like He heard me. But then, half a year later, something amazing happened when I attended a meeting in a church. There, a prophet approached me and started to prophesy over me. He said, "Do you mean it when you say to God, 'Use me'? Do you mean it when you tell Him, 'God, send me'? Do you mean it when you say, 'God, I will say what You want me to say'? Do you mean it when you tell God, 'I will go where You want me to go?' " Yes, he said the exact things I told God every morning for many months. And as he prophesied over me, I remember standing there, crying, saying, "Yes, God, I mean it." It was such a strong experience, and it showed me God always hears us even when we don't feel like He's listening. It also showed me that if we keep seeking Him, He will speak to us, even if it takes a long time to hear Him. So, I encourage you to ask, seek, and knock. Continue to do it because if you do, you will experience moments in your life where you will think, "Whoa, God does speak to me! Whoa, the Holy Spirit is working! Wow, God is answering my prayer!" Take the time to be quiet and seek Him.

WHEN YOU FAST...

Fasting is a very important part of getting to know God. Fasting means not eating (and sometimes not drinking any liquids) for short or long periods. When we look at the Bible, we can see that Jesus started His ministry here on earth after fasting for 40 days and 40 nights in the desert. And Moses, in the Old Testament, fasted twice for a 40-day period. We can also see many places in the New Testament where the apostles fasted. So, fasting was common in the Bible. Fasting can sometimes, as in the book of Esther, be three days without partaking of any food or liquid. You can fast once a week, or you can fast like Jesus did, for a longer time.

In Matthew 6, Jesus begins by teaching people how to give and pray and then continues to teach about how to fast. We can see this in Matthew 6:1-18 (NIV), which states:

"Be careful not to practice your righteousness in front of others to be seen by them. If you do, you will have no reward from your Father in heaven. So when you give to the needy, do not announce it with trumpets, as the hypocrites do in the synagogues and on the streets, to be honored by others. Truly I tell you, they have received their reward in full. But when you give to the needy, do not let your left hand know what your right hand is doing, so that your giving may be in secret. Then your Father, who sees what is done in secret, will reward you.

"And when you pray, do not be like the hypocrites, for they love to pray standing in the synagogues and on the street corners to be seen by others. Truly I tell you, they have received their reward in full. But when you pray, go into your room, close the door and pray to your Father, who is unseen. Then your Father, who sees what is done in secret, will reward you. And when you pray, do not keep on babbling like pagans, for they think they will be heard because of their many words. Do not be like them, for your Father knows what you need before you ask Him. This, then, is how you should pray:

"Our Father in heaven, hallowed be your name, your kingdom come, your will be done, on earth as it is in heaven. Give us today our daily bread. And forgive us our debts, as we also have forgiven our debtors. And lead us not into temptation, but deliver us from the evil one."

For if you forgive other people when they sin against you, your heavenly Father will also forgive you. But if you do not forgive others their sins, your Father will not forgive your sins.

"When you fast, do not look somber as the hypocrites do, for they disfigure their faces to show others they are fasting. Truly I tell you, they have received their reward in full. But when you fast, put oil on your head and wash your face, so that it will not be obvious to others that you are fasting, but only to your Father, who is unseen; and your Father, who sees what is done in secret, will reward you."

It is important to notice here that Jesus, in Matthew 6:2, says, *"... when you give ..."*, and in Matthew 6:6, *"... when you pray ..."*, and in Matthew 6:16, *"When you fast ..."* He did not say "if" you fast, but "when" you fast. Sadly, though, many churches today talk about giving and praying, but not many talk about fasting. Fasting is very important.

When God spoke to me and told me to go to Nakskov, it was at the end of a 40-day fast. He spoke to me on the thirty-ninth day of a 40-day fast where I drank liquids but did not eat anything. When God spoke to me on the thirty-ninth day, it changed my life. I have come to realize that when I fast, I see the biggest personal breakthroughs in my life.

Why is fasting so important? Well, try to imagine you have one white dog and one black dog, and they are equal in strength. Imagine you see them start to fight, and you want the white dog to win. So you decide to stop feeding the black dog, and you give more food to the white dog. Over time, the black dog becomes weaker, and the white dog becomes stronger. And in the end, because the white dog is stronger, it wins. This is what happens with our soul and spirit. When we give our soul (our flesh) what it wants, it will be strong. However, if we deny the flesh what it wants and feed our spirit instead, our flesh will become weaker and our spirit will become stronger. This is exactly what happens when we do not eat for a long period of time. Our flesh, when it is denied what it wants, grows weak, but when we pray, seek God, and read His Word, our spirit grows stronger. It is easier to receive dreams and visions from God while fasting, to hear Him speak to you, and receive breakthroughs in your personal life. Fasting is something very special, and I recommend that you take more time to learn about it. You can access our teachings about fasting on the Online "Pioneer School". There, you will find practical advice and biblical teaching about fasting.

HOW TO GROW UP

I have briefly mentioned the different spiritual levels (babies, children, and parents) in this lesson. We can read in 1 John 2:12 (NIV), how John addressed the spiritual babies/children by stating, *"I am writing to you, dear children, because your sins have been forgiven on account of His name."* New believers/babies in the faith need a lot of encouragement. They need to be encouraged over and over again. It is important for them to hear, "Your sins are forgiven" because they are young in the faith, and it is easier for them to experience fear and doubt. New believers need to learn how to walk in this new life. They need to understand that they will fall and make mistakes. When they experience a fight, they need more mature believers around them who can help them and say, "Come on, stand up again. Don't let Satan bring you down. God has changed your life and is continuing to do so. You fell and made a mistake, and it was wrong, but stand up again. Move on." Even if they tell you they don't feel forgiven, encourage them. "Your sins are forgiven. It's not about how you feel." New believers also need someone who can spiritually support them and help them understand the Word of God. It is important for them to read the Bible, but when they are totally new in the faith, don't just hand them the Bible and say, "Go and read it yourself." You need to take the time to explain the Bible to them. Show them what the Word says about righteousness, faith, repentance, and other basic things. It is important to recognize the babies in the faith because just like a baby in the physical world needs parents to survive, newborn believers need help from more mature believers to survive. They need help more than once a week. They need a family to come beside them.

When I first came to God, I wanted fellowship. I wanted more of this life, and I could not get enough. I needed more than just attending church once a week. I remember how I experienced attacks of fear and how I fell back into sin. I felt so condemned. When I read the Bible, I did not understand what it was saying. I praise God that He brought someone into my life to help me, my father-in-law. He was there for me and helped me grow. When we met to talk about the Bible, we would often sit down in his living room, on the couch, with our Bibles in our hands, and talk. I remember asking him so many questions about the Bible, and it was such a blessing to have him there to answer my questions. He told me about life with Jesus and encouraged me when I felt down. This is what new believers need: a family. A weekly sermon is not enough. They need a family who can spiritually support them and help them grow.

If you who are reading this book are new in faith, I want to tell you that when you struggle and sometimes experience fear and doubt or have fallen into sin again, we have all been there. It is important for you to rise up and be strong. Try to find people around you who can encourage you to keep going because it will get easier and easier to live this life. There is hope. Today, I don't struggle with that same fear, doubt, or sin as I did in the beginning. I have grown and am at another place in my life now, and you will grow, too.

We see John address young men in faith in 1 John 2:14 (NIV), which states, "...

I write to you, young men, because you are strong, and the word of God lives in you, and you have overcome the evil one." These "young men" John is referring to are people who read the Word themselves and have grown in understanding it. If you who are mature in faith have young men and women asking you questions about the Bible, it is important that you do not always giving them the answers. Instead, ask them what the Bible says in regard to their questions. Tell them to go home and read the Bible for themselves to try and find the answer. Introduce them more and more to the Bible, so they can read it themselves. Those who are young in faith, like the young men John is referring to, need to be encouraged. They sometimes need people to say, "Come with me. Let's go out on the streets together to share the Gospel. Let's go out and heal the sick and cast out demons. Let me help you do it." If you are a young man or woman in faith, I encourage you to start taking the responsibility of reading the Word of God yourself. You are strong and are now able to understand the Word of God. You need to start growing up so you can start leading other people to Christ. One day, you will find that you are no longer young in the faith anymore, but a spiritual father or mother with your own spiritual family.

John addresses parents in the faith in 1 John 2:14, which states, *"... I write to you, fathers, because you know him who is from the beginning..."* Here, John is referring to people who have been walking with God for many years. These are people who have gone through battles and desert periods and have endured attacks from the enemy, but are still standing firm. They have also led people to Christ, helped them mature, and provided an example to young believers of what it means to be a mature follower of Christ. Spiritual parents are very important. We need people who have been living with God for many years to help care for the young believers. So, if you are a spiritual parent, start inviting new believers to your place. New believers need you. They need a spiritual family in order to grow. They also need more than just attending church or a house church group once a week. They need people who can guide them and give them what they need so they can grow. If you are interested in learning more about this, you can check out the teachings about these spiritual levels on our Online "Pioneer School".

WHAT IF I DON'T HAVE FELLOWSHIP?

Fellowship is important. Acts 2:42 (NIV) states, *"They devoted themselves to the apostles' teaching and to fellowship, to the breaking of bread and to prayer."* We can read many verses like this throughout the Book of Acts, showing how the disciples met in homes to have fellowship. Like the apostles, we need to stand firm on the Word of God and to break bread and pray with fellow believers. You alone do not make up the body of Christ. Together with many other believers, we make up the body of Christ, and we need each other. This is because when a sheep strays away from its flock, it is easy for the wolves to come and kill it. We are in a spiritual war, and it is so important for you to have other believers around you so that when Satan comes and attacks you with things like fear, doubt, and sin, you are not alone but have help.

We all need fellowship, but what kind of fellowship? Many years ago, while I was still young in the faith, my wife and I attended church. But every time I went, it was like I could feel my faith being sucked out of me. Every time, it became harder and harder for me to live the life Christ called us to live. So, we decided it was best for us to leave the church. Despite knowing we needed other people to have fellowship with, we could not find anyone nearby. Eventually, we found a couple who lived two hours from us, and we decided to start meeting with them. So, once a month, we drove two hours to spend the day with them. Honestly, I got so much more out of spending the day with the right people than meeting with the wrong people once a week in church.

Something important to understand is that friends are like elevators. They can take you either up or down, but they never leave you in the same place you were before you met with them. You become like the people you surround yourself with. Therefore, it is important to find the right people to be with. Oftentimes, we need to drive far to have fellowship. Fellowship can be in a church building, a home, or even outside. It is not important where it is. What is important is that you share life and growth with people who are older and younger than you in faith. This way, you can both learn and give to others. This is very important for our spiritual growth with God.

If you are alone and don't know how to find fellowship, you can use *TLRmap. com.* This is a worldwide map people can put themselves on as a way to connect with other believers. I have seen many new fellowships start because of this map.

However, it is an open network, so anyone can put themselves on the map. Therefore, you must be careful. I recommend that you meet with people from the map and evaluate them. See if what they say and do is biblical.

It is important for you to find people with whom you can break bread, pray, read the Word, and grow. Like the physical family, God's design for us to grow spiritually is to have a father, mother, and siblings in faith. And just as a young boy or girl who does not have a family and lives on the streets would grow up with many struggles, we can also experience many struggles if we do not have a spiritual family to help us in our walk with God.

So, if you have no fellowship where you are, then drive for it. If you cannot drive to it, then move for it. We have no excuse not to have fellowship. I encourage you to find people who love Jesus and who are sincere in their faith. Spend time with them, learn from them, and mature in your spiritual walk with them.

THE CALL OF JESUS

LESSON SIX

Welcome to **Lesson Six** of the **Kickstart Package**. We have now looked at what a disciple is, the Gospel, how you can get born again, how to know God, and how to walk by the Holy Spirit. In this lesson, we are going to look at what Jesus called us to do and how we can serve Him.

When we repent, get baptized to Jesus, receive the Holy Spirit, and are born again, we deny ourselves and say "yes" to Jesus. We call Him "Lord" because we want to serve Him and obey His commands. What I love about the call Jesus has given is that it is for everyone. His call is not only for those people who are ordained in a church. It is not only for pastors and leaders. It is for you and me and everyone who is born again. The call of Jesus is not only something that happens inside of a church building, or something that only happens on a stage in Africa where people come to hear a sermon. The call Jesus has given us is for right now, wherever we are. His call is for you, young or old, man or woman, boy or girl. It is for everyone, and the moment you accepted Jesus and were born again, you said "yes" to His call.

Let's look at some of the things Jesus has called us to do. I would like to focus on what Jesus says in Luke 10. Keep in mind as we read Scripture from Luke 10 that Jesus is the same yesterday, today, and forever. This means that what Jesus said in Luke 10 was not only for the disciples who lived during that time, but also for the disciples who live today—you and me. Luke 10:2-11 (NKJV) states:

Then He said to them, "The harvest truly is great, but the laborers are few; therefore pray the Lord of the harvest to send out laborers into His harvest. Go your way; behold, I send you out as lambs among wolves. Carry neither money bag, knapsack, nor sandals; and greet no one along the road. But whatever house you enter, first say, 'Peace to this house.' And if a son of peace is there, your peace will rest on it;

if not, it will return to you. And remain in the same house, eating and drinking such things as they give, for the laborer is worthy of his wages. Do not go from house to house. Whatever city you enter, and they receive you, eat such things as are set before you. And heal the sick there, and say to them, 'The kingdom of God has come near to you.' But whatever city you enter, and they do not receive you, go out into its streets and say, 'The very dust of your city which clings to us we wipe off against you. Nevertheless know this, that the kingdom of God has come near you."

What Jesus said in these verses is still important for us today. When you start to obey His words here, it will not only completely change your life, it will also change the lives of the people around you.

As we have previously read, Luke 10:2 states, *"... The harvest truly is great, but the laborers are few; therefore pray the Lord of the harvest to send out laborers into His harvest."* This means there are many people out in the world who are ready and open to receive Jesus, but there are very few workers to go out and find these people. We also read how we should pray and ask God to send out the workers into the harvest. However, it's not enough to just pray for God to send workers into the harvest. We also need to go out. The harvest is not the problem. The workers, you and I, are the problem. However, I have good news for you. You can do something about it. You can go out into the harvest.

In Luke 10:3, we read, *"Go your way; behold, I send you out as lambs among wolves."* You may have seen a picture of Jesus holding a little, innocent lamb. In John 10:14-15, Jesus says, *"I am the good shepherd; and I know My sheep, and am known by My own. As the Father knows Me, even so I know the Father; and I lay down My life for the sheep."* Here, we know that Jesus is a Good Shepherd, and He takes care of His sheep. So why would Jesus say in Luke 10:3 that He sends His lambs out among wolves?

Imagine Jesus holding an innocent little lamb (which represents you and me). Suddenly, He sees a wolf. He notices the wolf wants to eat the lamb so He shows the little lamb that the wolf is hungry and wants to devour it. Then imagine Jesus setting that lamb down on the ground and saying, "I am sending you out." What kind of shepherd would do something like that? What good shepherd would take his sweet little lamb and send it out amongst the hungry wolves? I will tell you what kind of shepherd does this. It is the shepherd who goes with his lamb. This is exactly what Jesus promised us. He promised to go with us. When you, for the first time, pray for the sick, preach the Gospel, cast out demons, and baptize people in water and with the Holy Spirit, you will likely feel like a scared little lamb and think, "What if God doesn't come? What if people don't get healed? What if I do it wrong?" But, even when you feel like this scared little lamb, be bold and do it anyway. When you are obedient, you will see how Jesus is faithful and how He will be with you just as He promised.

Jesus, in Luke 10:4, states, *"Carry neither money bag, knapsack, nor sandals; and greet no one along the road."* Jesus said this because He wants to show us that He will provide for our needs. He wants to show us that when we go out into the harvest, He will take care of us, and we should not worry. In the next verses, Jesus says something very interesting. Luke 10:5-6 states, *"But whatever house you enter, first say, 'Peace to this house.' And if a son of peace is there, your peace will rest on it; if not, it will return to you."* What is a "son of peace," or as it is written in other translations, "a person of peace"? What are we supposed to do when we find this person? It is important to understand because when Jesus sends us out as lambs among wolves, He is sending us out to look for something specific— a person of peace. When Jesus started calling His disciples to follow Him in Matthew 4:19, He said, *"... Follow Me, and I will make you fishers of men."* Jesus still wants us to fish for men. He wants us to reach people for the Gospel. Jesus died for everyone, and His desire is to reach as many people as possible with the Good News of the Gospel. Therefore, we must fish for people and find a person of peace.

A person of peace is someone God is calling on and drawing to Himself. John 6:44 (NIV) states, *"No one can come to me unless the Father who sent me draws them, and I will raise them up at the last day".* So, no one can come to God unless the Father draws that person, and when he does, they are called "a person of peace." Many of the people we meet in our everyday life while we are out on the streets are not people of peace. They are more like the people we read about in Luke 10:10-11 (NKJV), which states, *"But whatever city you enter, and they do not receive you, go out into its streets and say, 'The very dust of your city which clings to us we wipe off against you. Nevertheless know this, that the kingdom of God has come near you'".*

So, we will meet two different kinds of people in our lives: those who are people of peace, and those who are not open to the Gospel. When we meet people of peace, we meet people who God is drawing, who are ready to follow Christ, and who want to receive our message. However, we will also meet people who don't want to receive our message. When we meet these people, we should shake the dust off our hands and feet and move on.

When you start to share Jesus with people around you, you will quickly see that what Jesus said in Luke 10 is correct. You will experience how some people you meet are open, and how others are not interested and might even think you're crazy for believing in Jesus. They might say, "God isn't real. Religion is bad. Evolution is the truth," or "Oh, you believe in God? Okay, that's good for you." And when you meet people who say these things, they are not interested and nothing you can say will touch their hearts. When this happens, move on. Shake the dust off your hands and feet and move on. Don't spend all your time on those people who don't want to receive your message. If you spend all your time with people who don't want to receive your message and only want to debate with you, you will not have the time to find those people God is drawing to Himself. Instead, focus on finding the person of peace because God wants us to find the people He's drawing, the people He has prepared to hear your message.

In Acts 16, we read how Paul met two different people of peace. The first person of peace was a woman named Lydia. We read how Paul and Silas went to Philippi and, in Acts 16:13-15 (NKJV), it states:

And on the Sabbath day we went out of the city to the riverside, where prayer was customarily made; and we sat down and spoke to the women who met there. Now a certain woman named Lydia heard us. She was a seller of purple from the city of Thyatira, who worshiped God. The Lord opened her heart to heed the things spoken by Paul. And when she and her household were baptized, she begged us, saying, "If you have judged me to be faithful to the Lord, come to my house and stay." So she persuaded us.

Here, Paul and Silas were out walking when they met a group of people who believed in God, but were not yet born again. When they met them, they told them the message of the Gospel. One person was especially open to their message, and her name was Lydia. We read how the Lord opened her heart upon hearing their message. Lydia was a great example of a person of peace. God opened her heart and drew her to Himself so she could receive the message of the Gospel. Not only did she receive it, but she also invited Paul and Silas to her home, and we see how everyone in the household was baptized.

Another example of a person of peace in Acts 16 is the jailer. Paul and Silas were in jail, and while they were there, they were worshiping God. Suddenly, there was a big earthquake. Their chains fell off, and their cell door was opened. They spoke to the jailer, and in Acts 16:30, the jailer asked them, "... *Sirs, what must I do to be saved?*" This is a really good question. When people ask questions like this, it shows they are a person God is calling. We read their response in Acts 16:31, which states, "... *Believe on the Lord Jesus Christ, and you will be saved, you and your household.*" So, Paul and Silas explained that in order for him to be saved, he needed to believe in the Lord Jesus. Then they went to his home, and we read, in Acts 16:32-33 (NIV), " *Then they spoke the word of the Lord to him and to all the others in his house. At that hour of the night the jailer took them and washed their wounds; then immediately he and all his household were baptized.*" Here we see another great example of a person of peace.

Today, we can experience the same things Paul and Silas did. We are called to obey Jesus. He said that when we find a person of peace, we should, as stated in Luke 10:7 (MEV), "... *Remain in the same house, eating and drinking what they give, for the laborer is worthy of his hire. Do not go from house to house.*" We also read, in Luke 10:9 (MEV), how we should, "... *Heal the sick who are there and say to them, 'The kingdom of God has come near to you.'* " We also need to cast out demons, as it states in Luke 10:17, "*The seventy returned with joy, saying, 'Lord, even the demons are subject to us through Your name.'*" As disciples of Jesus, we need to do it all.

I would like to share a story about a famous singer named Lou Bega. He is a great example of a person of peace. Lou was someone God was calling and drawing to Himself, and God really opened his heart to receive the message of the Gospel. He invited us over to his house and when we arrived, we sat down and ate, drank, and talked about life together. After this, we sat down in the living room, and I shared the Gospel with him, his household, and other guests he invited. Then we started to pray for them. One after another, they were healed, set free from demons, and received a new life with God. We baptized him, his household, and his guests that day in water and with the Holy Spirit. You can see more about this in our movie called, *"The Last Reformation: The Life."*

Lou Bega and his family are great examples of how we are called to find people of peace and obey what Jesus told us to do in Luke 10. Of course, ministering to people of peace can look different every time, as we can meet them in their home, or at a restaurant or another place. Despite the differences in location or how it is done, the call is still the same. Jesus wants us to find those who are ready to receive the message of the Gospel. Again, you and I are disciples, and we are here to learn to be like our Master. So, start by finding those people around you whom God is calling on. Find those people who you think are open to receive the Gospel.

Sometimes you may feel like God is leading you to certain people, but other times you just need to go to the people around you and start to talk about Jesus. When you do this, you will quickly discover who is a person of peace and who is not. If they are not open, move on to the next person until you find one who is open. You will eventually find those who say, "Wow, tell me more. I want to hear more about what you have to say." They will ask, "How do I get saved?" They will invite you to their house, and then you can sit down with them and share the Gospel. You may already know people around you who are ready to receive Jesus. Maybe that person of peace you are supposed to find is in your family, school, or workplace. Perhaps it's your neighbor, or the person living down the street you have only talked to a few times. Maybe the person of peace is someone who has faith in God like Lydia, but is not born again. It could be someone you meet at church or a prayer meeting who does not understand the whole Gospel or how we all need to be born again. If you ask God to speak to you and guide you to that person of peace in your life, I believe the Holy Spirit will put someone on your heart. When He does, go and visit that person and tell them about Jesus. You will see if they are a person of peace or not. When you find a person of peace, you will be so excited. There is nothing more amazing than seeing God change someone's life.

Remember not to waste your time with people who want to debate and tell you how crazy religion is. Just shake the dust off your hands and feet and move on from them. We read in Acts 13 how Paul and Barnabas shook the dust from their hands and feet upon coming to a place where the people did not want to receive their message. We see this in Acts 13:51 (NIV), which states, *"So they shook the dust off their feet as a warning to them and went to Iconium."* We can see how they moved on and went to another place called Iconium, and there, in Acts 14:1, we read, *"At Iconium Paul and Barnabas went as usual into the Jewish synagogue. There they spoke so effectively that a great number of Jews and Greeks believed."* Here we can see how Paul and Barnabas moved on and found many people of peace. Therefore, don't waste your time with people who don't want to receive your message. Find those people who are ready to receive.

Going out into the harvest and finding a person of peace was once new to me, too, and I had so many questions. As I stepped out in faith and obeyed the Bible, it became easier to recognize whom God was calling. It will also become easier for you when you step out and do it. You will start to meet people of peace who will say something like, "Wow, it is amazing that you stopped to talk to me now because, just yesterday, I asked God to send someone to me if He is real!" God is busy drawing people to Himself, and He wants to lead you to these people because He wants everyone to be saved.

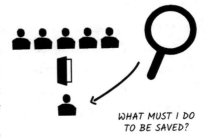

WHAT MUST I DO
TO BE SAVED?

A few days before I heard the Gospel for the first time, I looked up into the sky and said, "God, if You are there, come and take me! I want to know you!" I was truly a person of peace. I was seeking God, although I did not know Who He was. I thought maybe a UFO would come, beam me up, and fly away with me. I am so thankful for my friend Tommy who told me about God. Tommy could have said, "Oh, Torben is not interested. He doesn't want God." Instead, Tommy told me about Jesus, and I was so hungry, I wanted to hear more. I asked Tommy how he met God and told him I wanted to know more about Jesus. I heard the Gospel, repented, was born again and experienced a new life with God because Tommy was obedient to the call of Jesus.

I want to encourage you to start telling people about God. When you find a person of peace, share the Gospel with them. If you are unsure about how to share the Gospel, you are welcome to use all of our free resources. We have three free movies on *www.TLRmovie.com*, and many YouTube videos that share the Gospel. You are also welcome to use this **Kickstart Package**. When you find a person of peace, you can invite them to your home and show them the **Kickstart Package** videos. After they watch it and want to repent, be baptized in water and with the Holy Spirit, help them do this. Help them to repent, then baptize them in water and pray for them to receive the Holy Spirit. Lead them to Christ, and they may have friends and family who are also open and want to receive the Gospel.

It is important to keep it simple and obey what Jesus has called you to do. Just as we are called to find a person of peace, we are also called to heal the sick and cast out demons. We can see this in Luke 10. Healing the sick and casting out demons often go together. We can see from Luke 10:17 that Jesus' disciples both healed the sick and cast out demons. It states, *"... Lord, even the demons submit to us in your name."* They were so excited because they experienced the authority that had been given to them by Jesus to not only heal the sick, but also to cast out demons. Today, when you step out on Jesus' words, preach the Gospel, heal the sick, and cast out demons, you will also be excited. It is thrilling to see the power and authority in the name of Jesus. But Jesus, after His disciples were excited about the demons submitting to them, replied, in Luke 10:18-20 (NIV):

> He replied, *"I saw Satan fall like lightning from heaven. I have given you authority to trample on snakes and scorpions and to overcome all the power of the enemy; nothing will harm you. However, do not rejoice that the spirits submit to you, but rejoice that your names are written in heaven."*

I want to say the same to you. It is amazing to see people get healed and demons cast out of people in the name of Jesus, but don't rejoice in this alone. We need to rejoice that our name is written in heaven. Sometimes we pray for people who don't get healed, and sometimes we try to cast out demons from people who don't experience freedom. Therefore, it is important not to build our joy on that alone because if we don't see people healed or set free from demons, we will lose our joy. We need to build our joy on Christ and rejoice that our names are written in the Book of Life.

Healing the sick and casting out demons is not only for pastors, leaders, or someone with a special gift. It is for everyone who follows Jesus. Jesus makes this clear in Mark 16:17-18 (NIV), which states:

And these signs will accompany those who believe: In My name they will drive out demons; they will speak in new tongues; they will pick up snakes with their hands; and when they drink deadly poison, it will not hurt them at all; they will place their hands on sick people, and they will get well.

Here we read that these signs will follow those who believe. I want to encourage you to be bold. Go out there and find the person of peace. Share the Gospel of Jesus Christ and pray for the sick. When you step out on His Word, you will see that you are not alone, and you will experience people getting healed and set free. Remember, as I said in the first lesson, we are disciples/apprentices. We are here to learn to walk like Christ, and we learn by doing. It is okay if we do not look exactly like Christ now, but we should look more like Him now than we did last year.

Don't be afraid. I still remember when I first started doing all of this and how nervous I was praying for someone. I thought to myself, "What if they don't get healed?" or "What do I do if they get healed?" I prayed for many people who did not get healed, but I learned a lot. Eventually, I started to pray for people who got healed. Over time, it became easier and easier. I still remember the first time I cast out a demon. A woman fell down on our living room floor, and a demon started manifesting and screaming. I was so unsure of what to do because I had never cast out a demon before. However, the more I did it, the easier it became. I still remember the first time I found a person of peace. I shared the Gospel with them, and they wanted to get born again. I needed to baptize them, but I had never baptized someone in water before. I wasn't sure how to do it. I was afraid of doing it wrong and afraid of saying the wrong words. I also remember the first time I laid hands on someone to receive the Holy Spirit. I thought

I DID IT
XI X2 XS XIO...

↗ ↘

I LEARNED
I KEPT GOING

IT BECOME
EASIER

↖ ↙

I'VE DONE
THINGS WRONG

to myself, "What if they don't receive the Holy Spirit?" All of this was once new to me, too. I was afraid, but I learned by doing.

I want to encourage you to step out in faith and just do it. When you make a mistake, learn from it and move on. Making mistakes is normal. For example, I baptized people in water and later realized that they were not ready to get baptized because they did not fully understand repentance. I have also tried to cast out demons without seeing a breakthrough. I have prayed for people to receive the Holy Spirit, and it seemed like they did not receive Him. The important thing is that I learned from all of these experiences. I kept going, and I grew to know how to do it right the next time. So, for example, when you pray for someone who does not get healed, or does not receive the Holy Spirit, pray again. If you are afraid to pray for someone because you are afraid of saying the wrong words, know that it's not about your words. It's about your heart. Just keep going and obeying Jesus' call.

Many years ago, I remember training to be a fireman. At that time, we were learning First Aid, and there was a lot of new information we needed to process. At the end of the First Aid course, the teacher said something very important. He said, "Now that you have heard everything, remember one thing: the worst thing you can do is to do nothing." Why did he say that? Well, because there are people who focus too much on all the details (like how many times you are supposed to pump the chest or how many times you are supposed to blow air into the mouth), so they are too afraid to do anything, because they don't want to make a mistake. Those people are the ones who will do nothing, and they will not save one person's life. This is the same with ministry, the worst thing you could do is to do nothing. Ask God, "Who do You want me to reach out to? Who needs healing? Who needs deliverance? Who has already repented, but still needs to get baptized? Who is baptized, but needs the Holy Spirit? Who needs the full Gospel?" Let God lead you to people of peace, and make disciples of Jesus Christ.

QUESTIONS & ANSWERS

THE CALL OF JESUS

Lesson Six is very exciting, but there is so much more to say about the call Jesus has given us in Luke 10 than what is included in this lesson. I suggest you read another book I have written titled *The Call of Jesus*. In that book, I go into more detail. For example, I look at what the different verses mean in Luke 10. I believe that explaining these verses to new believers is crucial. They will not naturally understand that the harvest represents people, the sheep represent God's people, and the wolves represent our enemy and all those who are against us. So, if you show the **Kickstart Package** to new believers, remember to take the time to explain the meaning of the verses to them.

In *The Call of Jesus*, I discuss why Jesus says in Luke 10 not to greet anyone on the road. This can seem like a strange command, but the reason Jesus said this is because He wanted His disciples to remain focused on their mission and not become distracted. I also explain why Jesus said not to move from house to house when we find a person of peace. This is because we need to help them lay a foundation of faith in their life. We need to help them understand the gospel and be born again. Once they are born again, they are newborn babies who need milk. In that book, I talk more about what the milk represents, and how people grow into mature disciples of Christ.

Though there are many more things I could have shared in this lesson, I believe this lesson contains what is needed to encourage people to go out and find a person of peace, pray for the sick, cast out demons, and share the Gospel. I recommend to everyone who has watched the **Kickstart Package** to read *The Call of Jesus*. You can purchase the book on Amazon or directly on our website *www.thelastreformation. com*. If you don't have money to purchase the book, you are welcome to email us at *mail@thelastreformation.com*, and we can send you the eBook for free. You are also welcome to share the book with everyone in your house church once you are finished with the **Kickstart Package**. This will help you take a closer look at what Jesus has called you to do.

NOW THAT YOU HAVE HEARD, GO!

As I have previously mentioned, it is very important that you do not only hear about the call of Jesus, but that you obey it. After you have finished showing the **Kickstart Package**, I encourage you to take the people out on the streets to find a person of peace, pray for the sick, and share the Gospel. It's important to take the people out right away before the fear of going out on the streets has time to discourage them from going. It's so important for the people seeing the **Kickstart Package** to experience this life. As the disciples came back rejoicing because the demons obeyed them, those you take out will also come back rejoicing about the power of God, and the way God used them to heal the sick, cast out demons, and preach the Gospel.

If you have people who are more experienced with going out on the streets, then make groups where the more experienced people take the less experienced people out, to show them how it works. When you approach someone, you can say, "Excuse me, do you have any pain or something I can pray for you for?" If they say yes, pray for them and share the Gospel with them. Afterwards, take the time to share testimonies with each other about what everyone experienced while out on the streets before starting Lesson Seven.

We have many videos Online where you can see how we go out to find the person of peace, pray for the sick, cast out demons, and share the Gospel. If you are alone and too nervous to go out, use *TLRmap.com* to contact people near you who have more experience going out on the streets. They can come show you how to do it. It is important to overcome the fear and just step out and do it. When you step out and do it, you will be obeying Jesus Christ, and there is nothing more amazing than that. As I have previously mentioned, when you first step out, you will feel like a scared, little lamb. However, once you take that step of faith, you will also see how Jesus really does go with you, and you will be thrilled to see Him work through you.

FINDING THE PERSON OF PEACE

I encourage you to ask God who the people of peace are in your life. Oftentimes, people of peace are people we already know. So, take the time to pray and say, "God, please show me who I need to reach with the Gospel. Who is the person of peace?" It can be, for example, someone from your school, workplace, church, or neighborhood. As I have said in this lesson, the person of peace may already be a believer, similar to Lydia, but who still needs to understand the full Gospel, be baptized in water, or receive the Holy Spirit. The person of peace could also be someone who is seeking God but knows nothing about Him.

It is important to ask God daily who He wants you to reach with the Gospel. When you do this, He will guide you. Yes, He will put someone on your mind, and when He does, go to them and share the Gospel. When you start to obey Jesus and do this, you will see so much fruit. You are also welcome to show people the **Kickstart Package** and other videos on our YouTube channel or website. You can play the videos and use them as a tool to share the Gospel with people until you feel confident to share the Gospel on your own. The harvest is great but the workers are few, so we need to go out into the harvest and obey Jesus. I encourage you to use the tools we have made available to you, and to ask the people in your house church to take time to pray and ask God who they need to reach with the Gospel.

PICK UP SNAKES

I know many people try to discourage others from obeying Jesus' call and living a life consistent with what Jesus says in Mark 16:17-18 (NKJV), which states, *"And these signs will follow those who believe: In My name they will cast out demons; they will speak with new tongues; they will take up serpents; and if they drink anything deadly, it will by no means hurt them; they will lay hands on the sick, and they will recover."* There are some people who read this verse and say, "Yes, but in Mark 16:18, Jesus says that we shall also pick up snakes and if we drink poison that it will not hurt us. Should we also do that?" There are even churches in America that actually do play with snakes at their meetings because of what is written in Mark 16:18. However, this is foolish, as the Bible also says, in Matthew 4:7 (NIV), *"... Do not put the Lord your God to the test."* We should obey Jesus and heal the sick and cast out demons, but we should not put the Lord to the test. In Mark 16:18, Jesus is saying if you pick up a snake or drink poison, it will not hurt you. He is not saying we should do these things. Jesus is simply saying we should not fear if these things happen because they will not harm us.

We can see an example of this in Acts 28, where Paul went to Malta. There, a snake bit him. Paul just shook the snake off, and it did not harm him. The people there were amazed. He ended up praying for everyone on the island, and they were all healed. So, we should cast out demons, heal the sick, and preach the Gospel, and if anything should happen to us, in regards to dangerous animals or poison, we should not be afraid because He is with us. However, remember not to test God.

SHOULD EVERYONE GO OUT ON THE STREETS?

No, I don't believe everyone needs to go out on the street, but everyone should be a disciple of Christ and obey the call Jesus has given him or her. It is important to understand that going out on the streets is not the only way to find a person of peace. Finding the person of peace is something that can happen in our everyday lives. Healing the sick and casting out demons does not happen only out on the streets. It can also happen at your school, workplace, or when you gather together with family and friends.

We have seen a lot of fruit come from relationships. Many times, when people begin to obey the call of Jesus and start sharing Jesus with friends and family, they find people of peace. It does not happen only out on the streets. People you meet on the streets can be distant and skeptical because they don't know you or trust you. However, when you know the person of peace, they are more open and will trust you. Therefore, it is much easier for someone you know to receive your message. Going out on the streets to find the person of peace is a great idea when you don't already have someone you know and are reaching out to. It's also a great way for you to learn how to pray for people. It is easier to pray for those you don't know compared to people you do know. Once you practice praying for people you don't know and grow in faith and boldness, it will be easier for you to also pray for your friends and family.

If you are introverted and feel overwhelmed with going out on the streets, I still encourage you to go a few times. I recommend you go with someone who is more extroverted and whom you can learn from. When you see how it works and how God heals through you, you will grow in faith and boldness. Once you have done this, ask the Holy Spirit to lead you to work with the people you have in your network. When you find the person of peace in your network, ask them if they know any people of peace in their network. Then you will see the Kingdom of God grow from network to network.

I encourage you to use this **Kickstart Package** to set up small kickstarts in different homes. Those who are watching the **Kickstart Package** with you may also want to host the same Kickstart event in their home with their network and so on. This will help you continue to make disciples and obey the call Jesus has given all of us.

HEALING THE SICK: THE COMMAND OF JESUS

When we talk about healing the sick and preaching the Gospel, it is always important to start by looking at Christ because Jesus is the same yesterday, today, and forever. Jesus has commanded us to continue the work He started here on earth. If we take the time to look at Jesus and His ministry, we will see that He did not only preach the Gospel, but He also healed the sick. Matthew 4:23 (NIV) states, *"Jesus went throughout Galilee, teaching in their synagogues, proclaiming the good news of the kingdom, and healing every disease and sickness among the people."* We can see here that Jesus walked around preaching the Gospel and healing the sick. How did Jesus preach? We can see how He preached in Matthew 5, 6, and 7, where we read about the Beatitudes. How did Jesus heal the sick? We can see this in Matthew 8 and 9, where we read about the different miracles and healings He did. In Matthew 9:35 (NIV), we read, *"Jesus went through all the towns and villages, teaching in their synagogues, proclaiming the good news of the kingdom and healing every disease and sickness."*

When we look at the Gospel of Matthew, we can see how Jesus preached and healed. We read in Matthew 9:37-38, *"Then He said to His disciples, 'The harvest is plentiful but the workers are few. Ask the Lord of the harvest, therefore, to send out workers into his harvest field.'"* What does this mean? It means there are many people out there who need to hear the Gospel, many sick people who need to be healed, and many who need to be set free from demons. After He said this, He called His

12 disciples to Him and said in Matthew 10:7-8, *"As you go, proclaim this message: 'The kingdom of heaven has come near.' Heal the sick, raise the dead, cleanse those who have leprosy, drive out demons. Freely you have received; freely give."* We see later that the 12 disciples were not enough, so He called the 70. Then the 70 were still not enough for the harvest, so, before He ascended into heaven and sent down His Holy Spirit, Jesus said in Matthew 28:19-20, *"Therefore go and make disciples of all nations, baptizing them in the name of the Father and of the Son and of the Holy Spirit, and teaching them to obey everything I have commanded you. And surely I am with you always, to the very end of the age."* Here we see that the harvest is so large that Jesus commanded us all to heal the sick and preach the Gospel.

Jesus is the same yesterday, today, and forever, and we are still supposed to continue to preach the Gospel and heal the sick like He did. Like Him, we need to look for a person of peace, stay in their house, eat what they serve, heal the sick, and preach the Gospel. We see Jesus do these things in Matthew 9 when He met Matthew. We read how He went to Matthew's house and sat down to eat. And in Matthew 9:12-13, Jesus clarified why He was in Matthew's house by saying, *"It is not the healthy who need a doctor, but the sick. But go and learn what this means: 'I desire mercy, not sacrifice.' For I have not come to call the righteous, but sinners."* This is what we should do today. Nowhere in the Bible does it say we should only preach the Gospel or only heal the sick. Healing the sick and preaching the Gospel go hand in hand.

IS HEALING STILL FOR TODAY?

There are many people who say healing is not for today, and that it ceased with the apostles. However, I want to be very clear and say that this teaching is false and is not consistent with the Word of God. Many people also say healing is only for a few people with a special gift. However, this is also false and does not line up with the Word of God. Mark 16:17-18 (NKJV) states, *"And these signs will follow those who believe; In My name they will cast out demons; they will speak with new tongues; they will take up serpents; and if they drink anything deadly, it will by no means hurt them; they will lay hands on the sick, and they will recover."* We can see from these verses that healing is not only for people with a special gift. Since Jesus is the same yesterday, today, and forever, we know that His command to us has not changed either. Therefore, in the name of Jesus, we are still supposed to heal the sick today.

Yes, the Bible does mention a gift of healing. We read this in 1 Corinthians 12:28 (NIV) which states, *"And God has placed in the church first of all apostles, second prophets, third teachers, then miracles, then gifts of healing, of helping, of guidance, and of different kinds of tongues"*. It is important to understand that the job of all these gifts and callings is to equip the saints. We see this in Ephesians 4:11-12 (NKJV), which states, *"And He Himself gave some to be apostles, some prophets, some evangelists, and some pastors and teachers, for the equipping of the saints for the work of ministry, for the edifying of the body of Christ"*. We can see from these verses that there are people who have a calling to be an apostle, a prophet, an evangelist, and a teacher. There are also those with gifts of healing, helping, guidance, and different kinds of tongues. So, not everyone has the gift of healing, but everyone can heal. It's also the same with all the gifts. Not everyone has the gift of helping, but everyone can help. Not everyone is an evangelist, but everyone can evangelize. Not everyone is a teacher, but everyone can teach something. And not everyone is a prophet, but everyone can prophesy.

When I, for example, host a kickstart weekend, I am equipping the believers to go out and heal the sick. When I do this, I am using the gift God gave me to equip the saints to do the ministry Jesus has called them to do. I have a friend who is very prophetic, and He has been teaching me to become better in prophesying. However, just because someone can prophesy does not mean they are a prophet. Just because someone can teach does not mean they are a teacher. Just because someone can heal the sick does not mean they have a gift of healing. However, if someone starts to equip saints in, for example, healing the sick, then it is likely they have a gift in that area.

Do not focus on whether or not you have a gift. Instead, focus on obeying Jesus and what we read in Mark 16:17 will follow. Go out, preach the Gospel, make disciples, heal the sick, and cast out demons. Start to do what Jesus has called you to do and you may grow strong in a certain area. Then you can start to equip other believers to do the same. If this happens, then we can say you have a gift in that area, and it should be used to equip the saints.

You do not need the gift of healing to heal the sick. Imagine if we lived in a world where we could only do what we had a gift for. Let's imagine someone in the church was rearranging some chairs and asked you for help, and instead of helping them, you reply, "No, sorry, I can't help you because I don't have the gift of helping." Or imagine your kids came from home from school and asked you to help them with their homework, and you reply, "No, sorry, I can't help you because I don't have the gift of teaching." The idea that you can only do what you have a gift for is wrong and un-biblical. So, don't focus on the gifts right now. Just focus on being a faithful disciple and learning to obey the call of Jesus.

I recommend you to attend one of our kickstart weekends, where we focus on equipping the body of believers to obey Jesus. From these kickstart weekends, we have seen amazing fruit and an army of disciples rising up to heal the sick, cast out demons, and lead people to Christ.

START PRAYING FOR PEOPLE

Now that you have seen this lesson, start to pray for the people watching the Kickstart Package with you. Don't be afraid. Step out in faith and start. Everyone needs to start somewhere. Ask the people in the room if they have any pain in their body. Ask if any of them suffer from depression, anxiety, fear, and so on. Then, when you find someone with pain, ask him or her to stand up and then pray for them. What you say when you pray is not important. What matters is that you pray in faith and keep it simple. You can say, for example, "In the name of Jesus, I command the pain to go right now."

When you find someone struggling with something like depression, anxiety, or fear, lay hands on them and pray. You can, for example, say, "I command depression/anxiety/fear to go right now in the name of Jesus." Command it to leave them. If you have seen us do this in videos, then feel free to do it the same way as us. It is important to understand that faith is like a muscle, and the more you use it, the more it will grow. No one starts off as an expert in how to pray for people. No one starts off knowing exactly how it works or seeing 100% of the people they pray for get healed.

After you have prayed for someone with pain, ask them to check to see if they still have pain. If the pain is still there, just pray again. Sometimes we need to pray for people two, three, or four times before their pain is completely gone. When you pray for them the first time, sometimes nothing will happen. When you pray for them the second time, perhaps they may feel the pain reduce a little. And as you keep praying, you may experience the person saying their level of pain is continually going down. Just keep praying until the pain is completely gone. It is also different from person to person.

When you pray for people, it is a good idea to keep your eyes open. If you close your eyes, you cannot see what is happening to the person you are praying for. It is important to see their facial reactions as you pray for them because although you may start off praying for healing, it may turn into deliverance. Sometimes you may notice something is happening inside of them by their facial expressions. Sometimes they may start to breathe very deeply and look as if there is an inner struggle within them. When this happens, it is often demonic, and they need to be delivered of a demon. They may start to cough and eventually see something leave them. When I pray for deliverance, I often say, "I command every unclean spirit to come out right now, in the name of Jesus." Just take authority and command every unclean spirit to leave them.

On our Online *"Pioneer School,"* you can find many teachings, not only on how to heal the sick, but also how to cast out demons. I encourage you to watch these teachings. It is important to keep it simple. Look at Christ and have faith like a child. Start to use your faith muscle and let it grow. Pray for the sick and continue praying even if they are not healed the first couple of times you pray. We all experience praying for people who do not get healed because we are not like Christ yet. However, do not be discouraged. Just keep going, and you will see people healed in the name of Jesus. Keep sharing the Gospel with people and learn as you go. In time, you will start seeing many coming to Christ. Remember, we are all here as disciples, to learn how to walk like Christ. Maybe we are not there yet, but we should grow from year to year. We should look more like Christ this year than we did last year.

THE GOOD GROUND

Welcome to **Lesson Seven** in this **Kickstart Package**. I hope this Kickstart Package has been a big blessing for you thus far. I want it to transform your life. I believe many of you have learned so much more about the Gospel of Jesus, and how we, as His disciples, are called to follow Him. I also believe many of you have repented, gotten baptized in water, received the Holy Spirit, and started a new life with God.

Before I share this final, life-changing lesson, I want to remind you of what we have already talked about. In the first lesson, we looked at discipleship and how that when we say "yes" to Jesus, we say "no" to ourselves, and we choose to follow Jesus as His disciples/apprentices. When we say "yes" to Jesus, we will, over time, learn to walk, speak, be led by the Holy Spirit, heal the sick, and cast out demons as Jesus did. He is our Master, and we should learn to live like Him. Of course, we will make mistakes, and that is okay. It is okay that we don't look exactly like Jesus now, but as I have previously said, we should look more like Jesus now than we did last year.

In the second lesson, we looked at the new birth and how we cannot live the life Jesus has for us if we are not born again. We need to be born again in order to follow Christ and enter into the Kingdom of God. We looked at how we need to repent, turn away from our sins, and turn to God. We also looked at the importance of baptism, how it is not a symbol, and how baptism must come after repentance.

In the third lesson, we focused on the Holy Spirit and the importance of speaking in tongues. We also looked at how Jesus said in John 16:7 (NIV): "But very truly I tell you, it is for your good that I am going away. Unless I go away, the Advocate will not come to you; but if I go, I will send Him to you." Lesson Three also explains how the Holy Spirit will guide us into all truth and help us to walk as Jesus walked.

The fourth lesson speaks about the good news of the Kingdom of God. In this chapter, the Gospel is shared from the beginning to the end. We looked at how sin came into Adam and Eve and how they were thrown out of the Garden so they would not eat from the Tree of Life and live forever in their fallen state. We also looked at how Jesus came to earth as the new Adam in order to create a way for us to experience forgiveness and eternal life. One day, if we are born again, we will stand in the new heaven and new earth, eat from the Tree of Life, and live forever. We also focused on the importance of repentance, baptism in water and with the Holy Spirit.

In the fifth lesson, we focused on how we can know God through being born again and receiving God's Spirit. We are all called to have a relationship with Him. It is important to understand that we are not called to have religion but a relationship with the living God. We also looked at what it means to be led by the Holy Spirit and that God often speaks to us today.

Lesson Six talks about the call of Jesus and how this call is for everyone. Your age, gender, or how mature you are in faith doesn't matter. The call of Jesus applies to everyone. In this lesson, we spent time going through Luke 10 in order to understand the call Jesus has given us. We could see from Luke 10 what Jesus means by saying in verse 2 (NKJV): "... *The harvest truly is great, but the laborers are few; therefore pray the Lord of the harvest to send out laborers into His harvest."* We also looked at how we should find a person of peace and what we should do after we find them.

In this lesson, Lesson Seven, I am going to be sharing about the good ground. Here, we are going to look at the importance of obeying everything we have looked at throughout this **Kickstart Package**. It is not enough to just listen to the things that have been shared thus far. We need to obey them and follow Christ. Sadly, many of you will finish this **Kickstart Package** and forget everything you have heard. Others will receive Jesus' words into their hearts, and maybe start to obey them, but will fall away when persecution comes. Some of you will want to obey everything you have heard but will not be able to because you are so busy with life and all its worries. You will end up prioritizing those things instead of Jesus. However, I do believe there are some of you out there who will not only listen but also receive Jesus' words into a good heart. You are the ones who will choose to obey Jesus, doing whatever is necessary. Therefore, as you obey Jesus, you will see amazing fruit in your life.

As we look at this more in this lesson, I hope it will help each of you to become the good ground that will bear much fruit doing your Master's will. Let's start by looking at The Parable of the Sower found in Mark 4. Jesus states in Mark 4:3-8 (NIV):

"Listen! A farmer went out to sow his seed. As he was scattering the seed, some fell along the path, and the birds came and ate it up. Some fell on rocky places, where it did not have much soil. It sprang up quickly, because the soil was shallow. But when the sun came up, the plants were scorched, and they withered because they had no root. Other seed fell among thorns, which grew up and choked the plants, so that they did not bear grain. Still other seed fell on good soil. It came up, grew and produced a crop, some multiplying thirty, some sixty, some a hundred times."

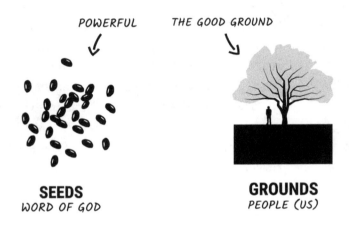

POWERFUL   THE GOOD GROUND

SEEDS   **GROUNDS**
WORD OF GOD   PEOPLE (US)

This parable speaks about a man who is sowing seeds. The seeds in this parable represent the Word of God. The seed (Word of God) is very powerful. It can bring freedom, forgiveness, and so much fruit in your life. However, the seed (Word of God) alone is not enough. It needs to fall on the right ground in order for it to produce fruit. In this parable, Jesus talks about how these four different grounds represent four different kinds of people. The seed is the Word of God, and Jesus is saying it needs to fall on the right ground (the right person) to be able to produce fruit. I believe if you take this simple truth we have looked at throughout this **Kickstart Package**, it has the power to not only transform your life, but also the lives of many people around you. However, in order for that to happen, you need to be the good ground that receives the Word into a good heart, obeys it, and doesn't give up when life becomes hard.

So what is the good ground? The good ground is people who hear the Word, receive it, and bear a lot of fruit. But what is fruit? What does it mean to bear good fruit? And how much fruit does God want us to bear? Well, I can start off by saying

Jesus wants us to bear a lot of fruit. In John 15:2 (NIV), Jesus states, *"He cuts off every branch in me that bears no fruit, while every branch that does bear fruit He prunes so that it will be even more fruitful."* This is very serious. He wants us to bear fruit, but what kind of fruit? Well, there are two kinds of fruit. First, there is the fruit of the Spirit that we read about in Galatians 5:22-23 (NIV), which states, *"But the fruit of the Spirit is love, joy, peace, forbearance, kindness, goodness, faithfulness, gentleness and self-control ..."* This is some of the good fruit we need to have in our life. If we walk by the Spirit and let God transform our lives, we should be producing these fruits. There is also another kind of fruit that comes by obeying Jesus' words. We can see this by what Jesus says in John 15:16 (NIV), which states, *"You did not choose Me, but I chose you and appointed you so that you might go and bear fruit—fruit that will last—and so that whatever you ask in My name the Father will give you."* Here, the fruit Jesus is referring to is people. He wants us to go out and bear everlasting fruits. He wants us to obey His call and win people over for the Gospel. Jesus wants everyone to be saved, and He needs us to go out and continue the work He started when He was here on earth. If we receive His words and obey, we will experience this kind of fruit in our life.

ALONG THE PATH 25%
▸ *NOT GONE INTO THE HEART*
▸ *WE SHOULD MOVE ON*

Now, let's look at the four grounds mentioned in Mark 4. Only one of the four grounds mentioned is the good ground that will bear a lot of fruit. In Mark 4:8 (NIV), Jesus speaks about this ground by stating, *"Still other seed fell on good soil. It came up, grew and produced a crop, some multiplying thirty, some sixty, some a hundred times."* Right now, you are one of these four grounds, and there is a 25% chance that you are the good ground. Mark 4:4 (NIV) tells about the first ground. It states, *"As he was scattering the seed, some fell along the path, and the birds came and ate it up."* Here we can see how the seeds did not go into the soil, and the birds came and ate them. In Mark 4:15, Jesus talks about this ground by stating, *"Some people are like seed along the path, where the word is sown. As soon as they hear it, Satan comes and takes away the word that was sown in them."* Here, we can see the seed in ground one represents those people who have not received the Word of God into their heart. Is that you? Are you ground number one? I don't believe so. I believe those who are ground number one are those who want nothing to do with Jesus. I believe these are the people Jesus was referring to when He told His disciples that when they enter a town and are not welcomed, to shake the dust off of their hands and feet and move on.

ON THE ROCKY PLACES 33%
▶ DON'T HAVE DEEP ROOTS ▶ PERSECUTION
▶ FALL AWAY / COMPRONISE

Let's say you are not ground number one. There are now three grounds left, which means that there is a 33% chance you are the good ground that bears a lot of fruit. In Mark 4:5-6 (NIV), Jesus talks about ground two by stating, *"Some fell on rocky places, where it did not have much soil. It sprang up quickly, because the soil was shallow. But when the sun came up, the plants were scorched, and they withered because they had no root."* Later, Jesus explained what this means in Mark 4:16-17: *"Others, like seed sown on rocky places, hear the word and at once receive it with joy. But since they have no root, they last only a short time. When trouble or persecution comes because of the word, they quickly fall away."* So, people who are ground two are those who have received the Word of God into their heart and have started to bear fruit. From the outside, they might look good, but when the sun, representing persecution, comes, they wither and die. The sun (persecution) actually reveals a problem with the plant (them) that we cannot see from the outside. It shows they did not have deep roots in God and because of that, when persecution comes, they fall away. Or maybe they don't fall away right away, but they start to compromise the truth for the sake of peace. Those who fall away because of persecution are ground two.

Persecution itself is not bad. People who experience persecution and are the good ground do not fall away. Instead, they fall on their knees and seek God even more. These people pray, seek God, and grow even more when they experience persecution. We need to understand that persecution has never been an enemy for the real church of God. However, those who are ground two are not willing to pay the price to follow Jesus, and they will fall away when persecution comes. Following and obeying Jesus is not easy, and Jesus has never promised us an easy life. In fact, He actually promised us the opposite. He promised we would go through persecution, we would be hated because of His name, and we would have to go through many trials in order to enter the Kingdom of God. It is important to understand the early church was made up of martyrs. They were willing to die for Jesus, and many of them did. If you would have preached our modern Gospel to them and said, "Give your life to Jesus, and He will fix your life and give you whatever you want," they would look at you confused and say, "What do you mean? My uncle gave his life to Jesus, and he is in jail." "My mother gave her life to Jesus, and she was beaten." "My cousin gave his life to Jesus, and he was burned alive." They would be so confused and think you were crazy. Over 90% of Jesus' first disciples were killed for following Him. But Jesus talks about the price of following Him in Matthew 16:24-25 (NIV), which states, *"Then Jesus said to His disciples, 'Whoever wants to be My disciple must deny themselves and take up their cross and follow Me. For whoever wants to save their life will lose it, but whoever loses their life for Me will find it.'"*

It costs everything to follow Jesus, but many do not understand this because they have sat in church their entire life without experiencing persecution. Maybe this is you or someone you know? You will see that when you start to obey Jesus and heal the sick, cast out demons, baptize people in water, and make disciples, Satan will hate you, and you will be a threat to his kingdom. Persecution will come, and many will fall away because many people are not ready to receive persecution and don't believe persecution exists in their country. However, Jesus promises that everyone who obeys Him will experience persecution, no matter where they live. Many people will be especially surprised to find out most of the persecution comes from people they know and love. It often comes from the church, friends, and family. I remember how hard it was when I first gave my life to Christ. My father, my co-workers, and even the church were all against me. Even people who believed in Jesus were against me, and they told many lies about me. It was very hard. Persecution is not only physical; it can also be mental or emotional. It is painful when people who were once your friends turn against you and, for example, spread rumors about you. Today, I have even experienced persecution from my own country and have had to flee to America. But, like Jesus states in Matthew 10:23 (NIV), *"When you are persecuted in one place, flee to another..."* Persecution is hard, and none of us like it, but you need to decide whom you will obey. Will you choose to obey man or Christ? Don't choose to be ground two. Keep going, and don't compromise. It is easy to just compromise for the sake of peace when people say, "I don't want you to baptize people in your bathtub," "I don't want you to have meetings in your home," "You are not allowed to pray for people! Who do you think you are?" But don't give in. When you experience persecution, remember this teaching and decide you will not be ground two. I often think of this teaching when I am persecuted, and I think to myself, "I don't want to be ground two; I want to be ground four. I will not give up!" And then I stand firm and continue doing what Jesus wants me to do.

AMONG THE THORNS 50%
▸ *RECEIVE IN THE HEART BUT...*
▸ *WORRIES OF THIS WORLD* ▸ *TOO BUSY*

So, let's say you are not ground two. There are now two grounds left, and there is a 50% chance you are the good ground that bears a lot of fruit. In Mark 4:7 (NIV), Jesus talks about ground three by stating, *"Other seed fell among thorns, which grew up and choked the plants, so that they did not bear grain."* Jesus later explains this in Mark 4:18-19 (NIV), which states, *"Still others, like seed sown among thorns, hear the word; but the worries of this life, the deceitfulness of wealth and the desires for other things come in and choke the word, making it unfruitful."* Ground number three is those people who hear the Word, receive it in their heart, and start to bear fruit. But then, something deceiving, which is growing all around them, chokes them, so they don't continue to bear fruit. What is this deceptive thing growing all around them? Well, Jesus says it is the worries of this world, deceitfulness of wealth, and the desire for other things. These things are the biggest problems in the church today.

When I look at the church, I can tell you what hinders them from bearing fruit. It is their house and job. I have met many young people who are in love with Jesus and who want to serve Him. I have met many who have dreamed about being a missionary and have wanted to travel all over the world to share the Gospel. However, one day, they fall in love with a big, fancy house, and they decide to purchase it. Then they decide to renovate and customize it. They decide to buy a nice car, too, and when they stand back and look at their big, fancy house and nice car, they think to themselves, "Wow, we are so blessed." However, they are not blessed. They are deceived because it is not their house nor is it their car. It belongs to the bank, and now they need to pay back the bank all the money they owe them. However, in order to pay back the bank, they need to work a lot. Then, when they come home after a long day of work and have to take care of things around the house, tend the garden, and care for the kids, they are tired and just want to sit down and watch TV. They are so busy they have forgotten about the dream that God gave them. Suddenly, twenty years go by, and they do nothing for God because they are too busy with life and don't have time for Him. These people are ground three.

The things in our life can kill the dream God gave us and keep us from bearing fruit. We need to be careful because these things that can distract us are deceitful. I know what I'm talking about because I have also experienced this. Some years ago, my family and I bought an old house and started to renovate and fix it up. At that time, I was busy with our house, car, garden, and my job. I was so busy and exhausted that by the time I came home from work and finished taking care of things around the house, I sat down on the couch, watched TV, and then went to bed. I did this from Monday to Friday. And when the weekend came, my family and I spent time with our friends and were busy tending to other obligations. Then a new week started, and I repeated the same thing over and over again, and time flew by. What happened to the call of Jesus? What happened to obeying God? What happened to seeking Him? Well, I didn't have time for it. I was deceived by the worries of this world, deceitfulness of wealth, and the desire for other things. However, one day, I was fired from my job, and although, at that time, I thought it was one of the worst things that could happen to me, looking back now, I can see it was one of the best things that happened to me. This is because when I could not pay my bills, I needed to seek God and ask for His help.

During this time that I was really seeking God, I realized how far away from Him I had grown. I had gotten so busy with the house, car, garden, and work, that I did not have time for Him anymore, and without even realizing it, I grew apart from Him. But when I got fired, I needed Him. So, I fasted and sought God. He started to work in my life again. I started to be led by the Holy Spirit, to see people get healed, lead people to Christ, and obey Him. When I experienced this, I knew I wanted more. There is truly nothing like obeying Christ and being led by the Holy Spirit. But I knew if my family and I wanted this life with God, we needed to be ready to pay the price to have it. I knew we needed to change some things in our lives, so we decided to move from our house into a small apartment. Why? Well, because then we would not need to work so much, and then I would have more time with God. We changed our whole life around to have more time with God. At one time, I only needed to work two days a week, and I had five days to spend time with God and serve Him. This time was amazing, but the truth is, we all have the same amount of time. We all have 24 hours per day. However, some people just prioritize their time differently to have time with God.

Those who are ground three do not have time to serve God because they are too busy with other things. (Or you could say they love the other things in their life more than Jesus, so they don't take the time to serve Him.) Don't be ground three. Don't let things deceive you and forget the call of Jesus. One day, we are all going to die and stand in front of God. And no one, while standing in front of God, will look back at their life and say, "I wish I would have worked more," or "Why didn't I get a bigger car or a bigger house when I had the chance?" Many people will look back at their life and say, "Why did I not live for Jesus? Why was I worried about what people were thinking of me? Why was I trying to please everyone around me instead of doing what Jesus expected of me?" Many people will also look back and say, "Why did I live for my house? Why did I live for my car? Why did I live for my hobbies? All of this just stole my time and focus away from the Kingdom of God." But on that day, it will be too late. When you stand before God, you will not be able to change anything. It is not too late today to decide whom you want to obey and what ground you want to be.

Don't allow persecution or anything else in this entire world to steal the call of Jesus away from you. Obey what you have heard in this **Kickstart Package**. When you make the decision to obey, Jesus will take care of you and help you. My family and I have gone through many hard times where we could have compromised and chosen to be ground two. However, we made a decision we would not be ground two, and we know it costs a price to follow Jesus. We have seen so much fruit, and we love serving Him, but we have lost many friends and even family. We have been kicked out of churches and were even rejected by our own country. We have had to live a simple life where we did not have many things other people have. We have prioritized God over a big, fancy house and, at times, chosen to live in a small apartment or even a motor home. It has been hard, but serving Jesus is greater than anything we will ever go through. I am not saying it is wrong to own a house. I am saying we need to prioritize our time correctly. Now, my family and I are ground four, and we are bearing a lot of fruit.

THE GOOD GROUND 100%
▶ *BEAR A LOT OF FRUIT*
▶ *X30 X60 X100 TIMES*

I don't know where you are in your life. Maybe you are already ground four and bearing amazing fruit. If you are, you are growing. You don't compromise for the sake of peace. And you take the time to obey God and go out to find the person of peace. If not, ask God what you need to change in your life to be the good ground, and He will show you. You can ask, "Are there places where I have been compromising? God, please show me if there are things in my life, like the deceitfulness of riches, worries of this life, and longing for other things that have taken me away from the simple life and call you have given me." Ask God to reveal it to you, and then change what needs to be changed.

I hope this lesson, together with the rest of the **Kickstart Package**, has blessed you. I really encourage you to go back and read or listen through the lessons one more time. I believe that if you go through it again, God will reveal things to you that you did not see the first time. I also encourage you to use this **Kickstart Package** to reach others around you. Be the good ground that bears a lot of fruit. Invite your friends, family, and neighbors over to listen to this Kickstart Package. If they don't want to, shake the dust off your hands and feet and move on. Look for others who want to listen to you. I also encourage you to find a person of peace, stay in their house, and show the **Kickstart Package** to them. When people repent, baptize them in water and with the Holy Spirit, pray for them to be healed, and cast out any demons. Then, you can disciple them. Be the good ground, and take Jesus' words into your heart and obey them.

I would like to end with Mark 4:8 (NIV), where Jesus states, *"Still other seed fell on good soil. It came up, grew and produced a crop, some multiplying thirty, some sixty, some a hundred times."* Make sure you are the good ground that produces a lot of fruit for God. Obey Jesus' commands and grow. Remember, we are here to help you. Together, let's follow Jesus as His disciples. We recommend you watch our free movies: *"The Last Reformation: The Beginning," "The Last Reformation: The Life,"* and *"7 Days Adventure With God."* You can also see the videos on our YouTube channel and teachings on *www.thelastreformation.com.*

I would now like to pray for you.

God, I pray for everyone out there who has seen this Kickstart Package. I pray that You will come with Your Holy Spirit, bless them, and touch their hearts. God, I pray that this word will become alive in them and that they will decide to be the good ground that bears a lot of fruit. I pray that this seed that has been planted by hearing these seven lessons will fall into good hearts and produce a lot of fruit. God, thank You for those out there. The harvest is great and the workers are few. I pray that You will send those who see this Kickstart Package out as workers into Your harvest and that You will lead them by Your Holy Spirit to find the person of peace. I pray that they will not only see a lot of fruit in their life, but that they will also see the Kingdom of God grow like never before. So, come with your Holy Spirit. I speak freedom, healing, and breakthrough over all of God's people, in the name of Jesus. Amen.

God bless you all. Be faithful with the call Jesus has given you.

— Torben Søndergaard
A disciple of Jesus Christ

QUESTIONS & ANSWERS

WHAT GROUND ARE YOU?

Now that you have read the lesson about the four grounds, I encourage you and everyone else to take some time alone to ask God what ground you are. It is easy to slip back from ground four into ground two or three, and we need to take up our cross daily, examine ourselves, and continue to be in Christ. The teaching on the four grounds is a great reminder for us when we experience persecution. It reminds us that we cannot compromise and fall back into ground two. It also helps us not to slide back into ground three when life becomes busy and full of distractions, and to stand firm in ground four.

Use this teaching to examine yourself to determine where you are in your life right now. What are the things you need to change to be ground four? You have the choice to decide what ground you want to be. Choose to be the good ground that bears a lot of fruit. If you are not the good ground, you can pray and say, "God, please speak to me and help me. Please show me what I need to change in my life in order to be the good ground that bears a lot of fruit."

We are all different, and some people may need to make big changes to be the good ground, while others may need to make small changes. Sometimes people may need to make a lot of small changes in their life. If this is you, it is important to remember that it is not something that happens all in one day. It takes time. Let the Holy Spirit continue working in you, change what you need to change, and you will end up as the good ground.

I have shared the four grounds teaching all over the world, and I often have people come to me and tell me this teaching changed their life. They often say that the first time they heard this teaching, they were ground two or three, but today, they are ground four and bearing a lot of fruit. I have also met people who tell me they were once ground four, but without realizing it, they slipped back into ground two or three, and this teaching opened their eyes again. They tell me they realize they need to repent again, and what they need to change in order to be ground four and producing good fruit again.

As I have previously talked about in this lesson, ground two represents those who experience persecution and fall away. It is important to understand that we will all be persecuted when we serve Jesus. That is part of the call He has given to us. We will suffer for His name's sake. So, what are we supposed to do when we experience persecution and suffering? Will you be ground two that compromises for the sake of peace, or will you be the good ground that does not compromise, even while going through persecution? People react to persecution in different ways. Some people stand firm and wait for it to stop, and although that is okay, there is an even better reaction. The best reaction to persecution is to rejoice. In Acts 5, we read about the apostles being persecuted for talking about Jesus, but then, in Acts 5:41 (NIV), we read their reaction, as it states, *"The apostles left the Sanhedrin, rejoicing because they had been counted worthy of suffering disgrace for the Name."* Wow, this is strong. We should rejoice when we are persecuted because we know that we have a great reward in heaven, and also because we have been considered worthy to be persecuted for His name's sake.

Do you rejoice when you are persecuted? Ask God to help you do this, and remember to guard your heart and keep it pure. In Matthew 5:44 (NIV) we read, *"But I tell you, love your enemies and pray for those who persecute you ..."* This is very important and something we need to do. Don't let you heart become bitter. We need to be very careful not to let this happen because when we experience persecution, Satan often comes and tries to put bitterness, hurt, and unforgiveness in our hearts toward those who persecuted us. We need to ask God to help us understand that persecution is part of God's plan and that we must love those who persecute us. Remember to rejoice because you are storing up treasure in heaven, and your Father will take care of you.

STORE UP TREASURE IN HEAVEN

We, as disciples of Jesus, need to get our focus back on eternity. We have become way too focused on this age, and not on the age to come. Jesus states in Matthew 6:19 (NIV), *"Do not store up for yourselves treasures on earth, where moths and vermin destroy, and where thieves break in and steal."* Here, He talks about how we should not store up our treasure here on earth. We should store it up in heaven instead. Where is your treasure? Where is your heart, and what do you invest in? Is your focus on this life and on getting as much out of this life as possible? Or, is your focus on Christ Himself and on honoring Him with this life and storing up treasures in heaven, not on earth?

Imagine you are hired at a new job and are told on the first day that your salary for the next ten years depends on how much you work on the first day. If you work a little, you will have a small salary, but if you work a lot, you will have a large salary. If you were told this, you would work as hard as possible on that first day so you would have a large salary for the next ten years. In the same way, what we do for Christ here on earth will determine our eternity. So, we need to focus on our eternity. Peter said in Mark 10:28 (NIV), "... We have left everything to follow you!" Jesus responded in Mark 10:29-30 (NIV):

Truly I tell you, Jesus replied, "No one who has left home or brothers or sisters or mother or father or children or fields for me and the gospel will fail to receive a hundred times as much in this present age: homes, brothers, sisters, mothers, children and fields—along with persecutions—and in the age to come eternal life."

Here, we see that those who give up things in this life, though they will experience persecution, will be blessed in both this life and the next. When we give up everything to follow Christ, we will have treasure stored up in heaven and be blessed in this life. So, I want to encourage you to obey Jesus' words, store up your treasure in heaven, and you will see that God is faithful and will bless you, both in this life and in the life to come.

DON'T WORRY

Jesus has given us the command not to worry. In Matthew 6:25-34 (NIV), He states:

Therefore I tell you, do not worry about your life, what you will eat or drink; or about your body, what you will wear. Is not life more than food, and the body more than clothes? Look at the birds of the air; they do not sow or reap or store away in barns, and yet your heavenly Father feeds them. Are you not much more valuable than they? Can any one of you by worrying add a single hour to your life? And why do you worry about clothes? See how the flowers of the field grow. They do not labor or spin. Yet I tell you that not even Solomon in all his splendor was dressed like one of these. If that is how God clothes the grass of the field, which is here today and tomorrow is thrown into the fire, will He not much more clothe you—you of little faith? So do not worry, saying, "What shall we eat?" or "What shall we drink?" or "What shall we wear?" For the pagans run after all these things, and your heavenly Father knows that you need them. But seek first His kingdom and His righteousness, and all these things will be given to you as well. Therefore do not worry about tomorrow, for tomorrow will worry about itself. Each day has enough trouble of its own.

I believe this command is so important for us. As a human being here on earth, there are so many things to worry about. We can worry about the future, our finances, the kids, and so on. But all these worries hinder you from looking at Christ and finishing the call Jesus has given you.

There have been many times in my life where I have experienced being overwhelmed with worries. But when this happens, I go for a walk, and I think about Jesus' words here in Matthew 6. I look around at the flowers in the fields and think about how Solomon was not even dressed like one of them. If God takes care of the flowers that are here today but thrown into the fire tomorrow, I ask myself how much more will He not take care of me? And then I look at the birds, and I ponder Jesus' words again and think about how the birds do not store away food in barns, and yet God feeds them. When I think about this, I realize He will also take care of me. When I meditate on these words, I realize I have nothing to worry about because He will take care of me. So, I encourage you not to worry, and to take Jesus' words in Matthew 6 and speak them out loud. Look at the birds and the flowers and ask God to open your eyes to help you see that when He takes care of the birds and flowers, surely He will take care of you.

People often worry about their kids when we talk about living this life for Jesus. My family and I have thus far lived a crazy life compared to many others. We have traveled all over the world, and we have never lived a safe, simple, and secure life. But I choose to live this life for Jesus and my kids. Our kids don't need a busy mother and father who go to church for two hours every Sunday. Our kids need a mother and father who are there for them and who can show them the real life with Jesus. So, don't worry about your kids. God will take care of you and your family. As stated in Matthew 6:33 (NIV), *"But seek first His kingdom and His righteousness, and all these things will be given to you as well."* Remember to look at the birds and flowers, seek God's will, and you will see how He takes care of the rest.

FOCUS ON JESUS AND NOT ON THE FRUITS

Jesus, in John 15:2, talks about how we need to bear fruit. It states (NIV), *"He cuts off every branch in me that bears no fruit, while every branch that does bear fruit he prunes so that it will be even more fruitful."* This is very serious, and we need to have fruit in our lives. We also need to remember, a branch does not bear fruit by itself. A branch needs to be connected to the tree in order to bear fruit. In the same way, fruit will not be produced in our life by focusing on bearing fruit, but by focusing on being connected to Christ and doing His will.

There was a time in my life where I was very focused on bearing fruit, but after not seeing any, I became very frustrated. However, when I started to seek Jesus, my focus shifted from how to bear fruit to how to be a faithful disciple, have a relationship with Christ, and obey His call. When I did this, I naturally started to produce fruit. Matthew 7:17-20 (NKJV) states, *"Even so, every good tree bears good fruit, but a bad tree bears bad fruit. A good tree cannot bear bad fruit, nor can a bad tree bear good fruit. Every tree that does not bear good fruit is cut down and thrown into the fire. Therefore by their fruits you will know them."* If someone produces bad fruit, the solution is not to say, "You have to produce good fruit." A bad tree cannot produce good fruit. Instead, you should help that person to connect with Jesus. You should introduce them to the call Jesus has given them and disciple that person. When you do this, you will see God change them, and they will naturally start to produce good fruit. Fasting is a very important thing to do when you want to grow with God. We know Jesus started His ministry after a 40-day fast. I also started my ministry after a 40-day fast. I encourage you to ask God when you should fast because fasting is amazing and so important. On our *Online "Pioneer School"* and on *www.thelastreformation.com*, you can find more teaching about fasting and how it can help you grow and see amazing fruit in your life.

CONCLUSION

We sincerely hope that both this book and the Kickstart Package have been a big blessing in your life. We are all very excited about this book and the Kickstart Package because it contains simple and biblical teachings. There is so much power in the seed of God (the Word of God). It is our prayer that this will produce an incredible transformation in your life, and that you who are not fully born again will understand the Gospel, repent, get baptized in water, and receive the Holy Spirit. It is also our prayer that you will all be good apprentices/disciples who start to live the life Jesus has called you to. We encourage you to share these teachings with other people. Invite people to your home, play the Kickstart Package, and host your own little kickstart.

We have made these teachings available to you to equip you with the amazing tools you need in order to see other peoples' lives transformed by the Gospel, and also to help them start producing good fruit. Together, let's serve Christ and see the Kingdom of God grow like never before. We have many free resources available, such as our teachings and movies that can be found on www.thelastreformation.com. If you have shown this Kickstart Package to a group of people, remember to ask them if they would like to host a kickstart in their own homes with their friends and family.

It is our belief and faith that this will go from home to home and from network to network, and that together, we will see tens of thousands of lives transformed, and an army of people rising up as true disciples who preach the whole Gospel and bear a lot of fruit.

God bless you all!

ABOUT THE AUTHOR

Torben Søndergaard

Torben Søndergaard is founder of The Last Reformation, a movement that has spread all around the world the last few years.

This movement is helping the Church come back to the life we read about in the book of Acts. They are training and discipling thousands of believers to spread the gospel and see people healed, delivered, and born again. They are doing that through their many training schools across the world and the 3-day kickstart weekends, along with the free online Pioneer School. Torben has written several other books and booklets and produced three movies that are available on DVD or on their YouTube channel. The YouTube channel has over 125,000 subscribers and has been seen by millions. Torben and his wife, Lene, have three children and two precious grandchildren.

See more on their websites:

TheLastReformation.com • TLRmovie.com

TLRmap.com • YouTube.com/TheLastReformation